I COULD HAVE PRETENDED TO BE BETTER THAN YOU

New & Selected Poems
by Jay MillAr

Edited & with an Afterword by Tim Conley

Copyright © 2019 by Jay MillAr
Afterword copyright © 2019 by Tim Conley

All rights reserved. No part of this book may be reproduced by any means without the prior written permission of the publisher, with the exception of brief passages in reviews. Any request for photocopying or other reprographic copying of any part of this book must be directed in writing to Access Copyright: The Canadian Copyright Licensing Agency, One Yonge Street, Suite 800, Toronto, Ontario, Canada, M5E 1E5.

Anvil Press Publishers Inc.
P.O. Box 3008, Main Post Office
Vancouver, B.C. V6B 3X5 CANADA
www.anvilpress.com

> Library and Archives Canada Cataloguing in Publication
>
> Title: I could have pretended to be better than you : new and selected poems / Jay Millar ; edited with an afterword by Tim Conley.
> Other titles: Poems. Selections
> Names: Millar, Jay, 1971- author. | Conley, Tim, 1972- editor.
> Identifiers: Canadiana 2019007132X | ISBN 9781772141245 (softcover)
> Classification: LCC PS8576.I3157 A6 2019 | DDC C811/.54—dc23

Cover design by Derek von Essen
Interior by HeimatHouse
Represented in Canada by Publishers Group Canada
Distributed in Canada by Raincoast Books and in the US by Small Press Distribution (Berkeley)
Author photo by Hazel Millar

The publisher gratefully acknowledges the financial assistance of the Canada Council for the Arts, the Canada Book Fund, and the Province of British Columbia through the B.C. Arts Council and the Book Publishing Tax Credit.

Printed and bound in Canada

for Hazel, Reid, and Cole

Contents

Author's Preface / 9

Part One: The Years of Stitches and Staples (1992-1999)

Cartographers World / 15
Poem / 17
Joe Brainard Is Dead / 18
Morning Sky / 23
A Fact / 24
Errata / 25
To My Illustrious Career / 26
[Yawning again, waking up again] / 30
[You make me realize] / 31
Space Travel / 32
Back Seat News / 34
[Maybe we weren't so unimaginable] / 35
imaginary tombstones / 36
[bad days always begin the night before] / 38

Part Two: Seriously Taken (2000-2014)

Tree Culture — Some Field Notes (by Conwenna Stokes) / 41
Trees (by Conwenna Stokes) / 48
Lysdexia in Sunlight (by Alex Cayce) / 50
Seasonal Drift (by Alex Cayce) / 51
Critique of the Dying (by H. Azel) / 53
In Another Shimmering Lifetime (by H. Azel) / 55
Perfectly Ordinary Dream #1620 (August 17, 1925) (by James Llar) / 61

Perfectly Ordinary Dream #1962 (September 17, 1985) (by James Llar) /
Perfectly Ordinary Dream #4127 (March 30, 1928) (by James Llar) / 65
What in the World is Coming to (by John Elliott) / 66
Fly Agaric (amanita muscaria) / 67
Destroying Angel (amanita virosa) / 68
False Morels / 69
As Seen from Above / 76
As Seen from Below / 79
7 Fungal Threads / 82
Fact's Mile / 90
Nearby, Lakes / 92
Carve / 93
Data / 94
Home / 95
Privacy / 96
from *The Small Blue* / 97
    36. dense joke
    72. drowned notions of passed
    75. bizarrely tunes itself
Lack Lyric I / 101
Lack Lyric IV / 105
Lack Lyric V / 109
from *esp: Accumulation Sonnets* / 113
    "forlorn falls of autumn"
    "oh so this is your sidewalk"
    "the bits of light that don't repeat"
    "the sun goes down how narrative"
    "star covered seams of church daze"
    "skim elk clop soda"
    "in the future manifesto"
Lake Ontario Suite / 120
On Vocal Technique / 125

Woods Pages / 130
Lift / 142
The Lyrics to Your Next Hit Single / 143
More Trouble with the Obvious / 147
Timely Irreverence / 148

Part Three: New Poems (2014-18)

On Time / 151
Gathered for the Purpose / 154
Conceptual Poetry / 156
A Sentient Being Rises from the Sea / 157
The Shiny Things / 159
The Nature / 165
Our Journey from Silence / 167
Another Poem About Time Written at the Onset of Middle Age / 169
How Light Pours from the Darkness / 171
Off in the Distance / 172

Afterword by Tim Conley / 173
Books by Jay MillAr / 183
Notes to the Poems / 186
Acknowledgements / 190
About the Author / 192

Author's Preface

How meaningful and strange to find oneself, at the age of forty-eight (am I really that young?), to have a selection of poems that spans my entire life as a poet, generously and thoughtfully chosen by my long-time friend and reader Tim Conley. I can say *meaningful* even if it is a more personal and intimate sense of the word, and I can say *strange* because time is a curious beast, and poetry is a serious joke. What does it mean to become witness to thread-lines that stretch back more than a quarter of a century, to see the various phases of one's work that emerged over the years? To look through the timeframe of this book I can see that I have been quietly obsessed with expression, and I can see influence — natural history, the New York School, CanLit 101, the CanLit anti-establishment — they are all visible. And though lifted from the pages of books and readings, the phases I see herein also have a lot to do with individuals I was involved with at the time. And maybe it's creepy: I can actually see these people in different poems. Some of them are people I no longer associate with. And this means I was not only thinking, "What's next?" but I was also thinking something along the lines of "Who's next?" even if it was unconscious. Or better yet "Who's worth keeping?" I'm still unsure if such acts of moving on were because of my engagement with poetry, or with my role as a publisher, both of which morphed over the years. The latter does require a unique relationship with poets, one that is different when it is poet to poet.

Regardless, I can acknowledge that my career as a poet has existed exactly the same length of time as my career as a publisher, and the two sides have always had a relationship, since I have often published my own work, right from the beginning.

The great exception to the flux and roll of time with regard to writing is Hazel, a beautiful someone I met at a Surrealist Film Festival in London Ontario only a few months after publishing my first chapbook. The day after our initial encounter I stopped by the house in which she lived with a few friends to ask her out, and discovering she was not at home, left her a copy of *Uranium Kisses Will Knock Your Socks Off* as a calling card. I remember feeling awkward as I walked back to the apartment that I was subletting from bill bissett on Richmond Street, because I liked Hazel a lot and knew that there was a poem in that chapbook dedicated to another girlfriend. But I also knew, even then, that the poem was entirely plastic, was about breaking up in an immature way, and borrowed heavily (to the point of imitation) from a poem by Phil Hall that I had stumbled upon in one of his books at the university library. Hazel didn't say anything about it during our hours-long conversation on the phone the next day. Instead she told me that she was amazed that poets still walked the earth, having believed, until receiving my chapbook and speaking with me, that poets had died out after the Romantic period. This certainly warmed me to her right away — she believed I was a poet. We have been together ever since, having moved to Toronto in the early 90s, going to school together — she for dance, myself for literature — getting married and having children who are themselves a constant inspiration. Together we continue to live what I can only refer to as The Dream. So even if there are shifts and phases to my work, and people who have come and gone, there is also a serious constancy from the beginning. To see both in these pages is thrilling and bewildering.

Lyn Hejinian says writing is an aid to memory, and I can't help but see a world around each poem that no one reader could possibly know. For instance, the basement apartment Hazel and I rented on Northumberland Street, or thoughts that bubbled up while I was hiding out in the stacks of the Scott Library at York University, or poems I continue to associate with the blue Norco bicycle I rode everywhere in the 1990s. Even a poem written while sitting in the back seat of a car as we drove north with friends to go camping at Arrowhead Provincial Park has shadows that are important, but more to me than anyone else. I mean, there is the poem for all to see in their own way, but to have an opportunity to revisit moments from my past that would have been completely forgotten without the poem is truly a gift. Hence the cliché of surprise. Surprise! Tim has done his homework — some of the poems in this volume were published in editions of as few as ten copies. Even I — the author of these poems — had forgotten about some of them until now, and until working on this volume with Tim I had a habit of imagining my oeuvre as only a handful of poems, self-categorized greatest hits. Very few of those poems are actually in this collection.

What is surprising to me, especially in the earlier work, is to see poems written with such youthful abandon — there is a lot of work by someone who was simply "going for it" — young and foolish enough to simply think it's ok to go on his nerve. It reminds me of something to which I can never return, and there are days that I long to recapture that energy. Regardless, it is significant that these very early poems suggest attitudes that continue throughout the rest of the book — shifts from poems that are very much "present" to others that wax nostalgic. Some of the work is systematic; other pieces are spontaneous free-form expression. Some are abstract poems;

others are confessional, bordering on journal entries with line breaks. Such blatant disregard for focus has undoubtedly placed me everywhere and nowhere as a poet.

When I told my parents in the early 90s that I was going to move to Toronto to become a poet they were naturally worried for me — saying such a thing to one's parents is pretentious and, well, stupid. But instead of getting in my face about it they let me run off willy-nilly, chasing a girl, chasing a dream. And all these years later they don't hesitate to let me know what an interesting life I seem to lead and how proud they are of the world Hazel and I have built together. Which is very nice, since I have never been in it to win it. I have been in it to do it; whatever successes have come to pass are the delicious burdens we now carry. And within that, what I find most satisfying in this collection is seeing very clearly a relationship between poetry and life, two entities that have very little to do with each other in a practical sense, yet should always be same thing. I'm very pleased I can see it. I hope you can, too.

Part One

The Years of Stitches and Staples
(1992-1999)

cartographers world

invisible lines

drawn on the backs of brains
pinpoint everything existing
in this world

travelling counter clockwise
unseen meridians cause
time to move forward

dotted borders
divide and conquer

slicing the earth
like a butchered cow
labelling each cut with

a mine
or a
yours

yet within this severed chimera
of plant land mass animal water flesh
i find my home is located
exactly between
north south east & west
in a moment i call now

i can find it

wherever
whenever i am

Poem

Frank O'Hara has egg yolk on him.
It happened this morning. Around seven.
It happened because last night I
thought I might get drunk & I did &
now I feel perfectly disgraceful &
hungry so hungry my heart is bleating
too fast much too fast & all
the horrible tummy bumbles demand
that I should make a fried egg sandwich
which I did & now I have it in my hands
as I take my egg shell stomach for a walk
over to the table & sit down with
the very collected Frank O'Hara.
AND THEN IT HAPPENED
One bite & squirt! egg yolk all over
Frank. Poor Frank. But man was it yellow
a new form of plastic enamelled as
life can get the morning after &
feeling perfectly disgraceful as I was
I wanted more of the lovely yellow
plastic coating I wanted it to drip
from the ceiling & into my hair I
wanted to open the door to see a great
enamel sun in a yellow sky so I took
another bite & then another big one
O could my stomach ever be so peaceful
as the yellow glob of life that
somehow landed on Frank's word: "begin"?

Joe Brainard Is Dead

I am sad because Joe Brainard is dead.
I am drunk because Joe Brainard is dead.
I am smoking cigarettes again because Joe Brainard is dead.
I am pissed because Joe Brainard is dead.
I am beautiful so pee pee on you because Joe Brainard is dead.
I am the Eglinton Subway is dead because Joe Brainard is dead.
I am Yorkdale is dead because Joe Brainard is dead.
I am wealthy now because I have two of his books because Joe Brainard is dead.
I went to bed last night & dreamed like ink because Joe Brainard is dead.

I am awake in another day now because Joe Brainard is dead.
I have a hangover because Joe Brainard is dead.
I am a loser because he died months ago & I just found that out because Joe Brainard is dead.
I am wondering exactly what it is like to be actually dead because Joe Brainard is dead.
I am thinking a lot about death because Joe Brainard is dead.
I am trying to come to terms with death because Joe Brainard is dead.
I am eating spaghetti noodles without sauce because Joe Brainard is dead.
I acted perfectly disgraceful last night because Joe Brainard is dead.
I am almost single because Joe Brainard is dead.
I am skipping my classes today because Joe Brainard is dead.
I am slowly remembering last night in very tiny isolated details because Joe Brainard is dead.
I am alive because Joe Brainard is dead.
I am thinking Frank is dead Ted is dead Edwin is dead Jack is dead Grandma is dead Grampa is dead Chris is dead & now Joe is dead because Joe Brainard is dead.

I have no money because Joe Brainard is dead.
I am writing this poem because no reason no because Joe Brainard is dead.
I am wondering how Kenward is doing because Joe Brainard is dead.
I am wondering how Kenneth is doing because Joe Brainard is dead.
I am wondering how Ron is doing because Joe Brainard is dead.
I am wondering how Rob is doing because Joe Brainard is dead.
I am wondering how Hazel is doing because Joe Brainard is dead.
I am wondering how Stefan is doing because Joe Brainard is dead.
I am wondering why no one told me that Joe Brainard was dead because Joe Brainard is dead.
I am not going to meet him & say "Hi Joe!" because Joe Brainard is dead.
I am looking at his picture & he is smiling that quirky skinny Joe Brainard smile with a cigarette because Joe Brainard is dead.

I awake in another day now because Joe Brainard is dead.
I feel fine today & I'm hungry too because Joe Brainard is dead.
I dreamed last night a cop shot me in the leg because Joe Brainard is dead.
I remember reading somewhere that Joe Brainard smoked four packs of cigarettes a day because Joe Brainard is dead.
I remember that I used to like to eat Cheerios with at least half a cup of brown sugar on them because Joe Brainard is dead.
I remember that Joe Brainard wasn't afraid one bit of cancer, not one bit, because Joe Brainard is dead.
I remember when Stuart told me that Joe Brainard was dead I thought he had died of cancer because Joe Brainard is dead.
I remember that I am afraid of being dead for as long as I can remember because Joe Brainard is dead.
I remember all the times I got stoned because Joe Brainard is dead.
I remember putting the car in the ditch when I was nineteen because Joe Brainard is dead.
I remember drinking 3 cups of black coffee this morning because Joe Brainard is dead.

I remember reading "I REMEMBER" out loud to Rob Lemon because Joe Brainard is dead.

I remember I pissed off Hazel last night because I was pissed because Joe Brainard is dead.

I remember reading "THE UNFRIENDLY WAY" on the 106A bus to York University in springtime because Joe Brainard is dead.

I remember when Stuart told me that Joe had died I thought he died of cancer.

I remember travelling to NYC by bus in December wondering if I would run into Joe Brainard but I couldn't have because Joe Brainard was dead because Joe Brainard is dead.

I remember Stuart saying matter-of-factly "He died of AIDS."

I remember reading "THE BANANA BOOK" & laughing my ass off because Joe Brainard is dead.

I remember nothing in particular because Joe Brainard is dead.

I remember yesterday looking at his picture & he was smiling that quirky skinny Joe Brainard smile with a cigarette because Joe Brainard is dead.

I am awake in another day now & Joe Brainard is dead.

I am thinking "AIDS sucks" because Joe Brainard is dead.

I am listening to ABBA's Greatest Hits & Joe Brainard is dead.

I am suddenly remembering I dreamed last night of my father's death & Joe Brainard is dead.

I wish I could be as straight forward as Joe Brainard was in his journals & poems & visual work because Joe Brainard is dead.

I am writing a sonnet in memory of Joe Brainard because Joe Brainard is dead.

   I write:

      Coming up another battle in the fight against AIDS
      Coming up another battle in the fight against AIDS
      Coming up another battle in the fight against AIDS

Coming up another battle in the fight against AIDS
Coming up another battle in the fight against AIDS
Coming up another battle in the fight against AIDS
Coming up another battle in the fight against AIDS
Coming up another battle in the fight against AIDS
Coming up another battle in the fight against AIDS
Coming up another battle in the fight against AIDS
Coming up another battle in the fight against AIDS
Coming up another battle in the fight against AIDS
Coming up another battle in the fight against AIDS
Coming up another battle in the fight against AIDS

I am awake now in another day now & Joe Brainard is dead.
I am looking at that sonnet & thinking it's ridiculous because Joe Brainard is dead.
I want everyone to notice the Shakespearean form of that sonnet because Joe Brainard is dead.
I am trying to remember why I'm still writing this poem & Joe Brainard is dead.
I take a sip of my coffee to find it is cold & Joe Brainard is dead.
I look outside & I realize that it's totally raining today in T.O. & Joe Brainard is dead.
I look at the wall & I think "Joe is dead" because Joe Brainard is dead.
I look back a few pages & think to myself "I could go on forever" because Joe Brainard is dead.
I don't smoke any more & Joe Brainard is dead.
I don't drink any more & Joe Brainard is dead.
I don't feel like telling my cats to shut up any more & Joe Brainard is dead.
I don't have AIDS & Joe Brainard is dead.
I think about the three people I have met who have AIDS & I'm amazed to remember that all three of them are tall & skinny because Joe Brainard is dead.

I think "nothing in particular" because Joe Brainard is dead.
I am thinking thank you Stu & fuck you too for telling me Joe Brainard is dead.
I am thinking thank you Stu & fuck you too a second time for telling me Joe Brainard is dead.
I would be thinking thank you Stu & fuck you too a third time but instead I am thinking it would be nice if people could live forever because Joe Brainard is dead.
I am thinking life is wonderful & strange because Joe Brainard is dead.
I am thinking some people do live forever because Joe Brainard is dead.
I look at his picture & he is smiling that quirky skinny Joe Brainard smile because Joe Brainard is dead.

  I finally think: "Me & everyone else stop breathing, thinking:

> roses are red
> violets are blue
> life sure is weird
> & then you die

        & Joe Brainard is dead."

Morning Sky

Strange unpronounceable red outside
of the birds (Erik Satie was of
the birds, knew the plenitude of
clouds) wakes with a mysterious roar

the sun shoots out rays of red, orange,
blue & gold, & we are told our size,
somewhat larger than a squirrel
far less interesting than our own train

of thought speaks directly out of (time)
gathering a language no one tried to
learn (Erik Satie knew the lurch and
stretch of time) makes us so very small

just to wake us, just to make us small, "we
lay at the bottom of a strange ocean, in bed
where the trees were pure sexual beings, swaying
in our heads & your breath was the smell

and Satie was the sound of the sky, slow
moving, promising whatever came to mind"

A Fact

    they have severe difficulties
    when it comes to investigating
    the kind of tiny nipples in the
    radiation that would have to
    be there to explain the existence
    of galaxies & ourselves

Errata

page 1; line 3, "automatic writing" should read "collective vomiting".
page 1; second last sentence should read "This is an attempt to make a statement & to suggest that this is the way one should write poetry."
page 2; line 5, "collective unconscious" should read "space aliens".
page 3; line 18, "several odd photos" should read "several odd dildos".
page 3; line 22, "spoken to" should read "hit in the head".
page 4; title, "FAILURE" should read "RAINBOWS".
page 6; line 6, "delicate Ukranian hands" should read "baseball bats".
page 7; line 5, "bright lights" should read "distracted hookers".
page 7; stanza 2; line 5, "burning me" should read "feeding me".
page 8; line 3, "cold rain" should read "cold gravy".
page 9; section b; line 3, "legs" should read "pots & pans".
page 10; line 9, "swimming" should read "spitting".
page 10; stanza 2; line 2, "shit" should read "meal".
page 11; title, "SPELLING BEE" should read "veal".
page 12; line 4, "ignoring the television" should read "washing the microwave".
page 13; there should be no right-hand parenthesis.
page 14, there is no page 14.

To My Illustrious Career

I moved to Toronto so I could kick
your ass. Where I came from I delivered
papers as a child, I mean as a young
man, in the half-light of morning, wearing
knee-highs, so you could say I brought news both
good & bad to people, but mostly it
was just terrible since the paper was
no good. But I kept it up, & did a
lot of kid things I can't quite remember
any more. I cleaned stalls for money, sold
tickets, went to school & learned, that kind of
thing. I won girls & lost them too, but I'll
admit to you right now I mostly lost.
And I loved show & tell because I got
to be in charge for those five brief minutes.
Otherwise, suburbia was somewhat
uneventful, which led me to certain
narcotic afternoons & evenings, which
I liked better because there was no hang
over. And the funny pages always
gave me something to do, them & tv.
I thought once or twice about writing the
words on paper, but it wasn't the right
time. And eventually it all led
me somewhere & I fell in love with her
too & decided to let it all go.
So I disappeared, reappeared, & found
myself here, when everything was happening
at once. When it came time to write things down,

I got really excited, not that this
helped any. Soon, I discovered New York
City. I suddenly misplaced myself,
calling home "T.O." because it sounded
closer to "The Heart" of the matter, while
in my heart I misplaced her brilliant red
hair that was on the pillow next to mine.
She stuck with it though, while the sound of the
ambulances raced back & forth across
my typewriter, scattering all of my
hallmark cards from east to west. In response
I kicked your ass a little harder, &
sometimes I got a good punch, right between
the eyes, seeing the words racing, wasting
themselves, turning somersaults in the air
just to the left or right of you. She
watched me make an idiot of myself
the whole time, just watching, turning up her
eyes both in awe & an amazingly
clear form of annoyance. I gained my strange
illusion of an American five a.m.
I wondered: "why must it always
be winter there, with a dirty window
opened to the lightly falling snow since
the lousy steam heater keeps the house too
hot?" I wondered about all that, so I
wrote it down in my secret journals, or
at least I do now. I've only seen it
once, & that was from the back seat of a
bus, as I looked over her red hair, &
despite all of the old grey Christmas-time
geometry shooting up into the

air across the river, it felt very
warm. So after a week or so I came
home & sat around on my ass a lot,
sometimes on the john, sometimes now, & when
it started to rain again, I got on
with things. I did the dishes, took out the
trash, played with the cats, ran my fingers through
her hair, did whatever came to mind &
I discovered there were other cities
around the world with their little things to
offer — the back step among them, the grass
in the yard, the mailbox itself as it
hung next to the door & other places.
Places that had never noticed me too.

I admit I got really tired of you,
sometimes occasionally, & I have
to apologize: all that war-paint was
simply a display, but I continued to
reel it home, trying to remember that
when we die you can't sleep in any more.
And that was enough to keep me going.
I still got excited from time to time,
got hired & fired in the usual chain
of events, but it was mostly to keep
going. It got dark & then light, the sun
came & went, & it got ready to snow
again. I appeared here & there around
the apartment, but mostly it was here.
Sometimes I accompanied myself. I
got some new clothes, went super low-tech, gave
up my silly notion of kicking your

ass & learned to accept you naturally,
let you come & go among the papers
I deliver with a certain excitement.
& I still get really excited when
you come knocking. Other times I just turn
on the radio & listen to some
of that old music coming to me from
across the room, & it brings me back into
where I am now, thinking of you & her
brilliant red hair, which is coming home with
her to me at this particular moment
while a dinner I am cooking feeds its
way into the stove I cooked up with words.

Yawning again, waking up again
Hearing your breath in my ear again

Quiet moments of morning before the morning begins again & you
Zoom out into the working world again

I will sit in a chair again
Reading another book again

Again I will write the word again again
Just knowing it will repeat again with a new kind of utterance puts
    me at ease again

Some sun in the window again makes me
Believe in today again

You make me realize how my attention goes around in a cycle, one minute I'm
    really interested in making books, the next I'm tired from the effort
Hearing my own thoughts from one week to the next without stopping gets tiring

Quit breaking everything around me, you forces I have nothing to do with, first it
    was the migraine headache during which I broke the left arm of my glasses,
    then the bolt holding the handlebars onto my bike snapped after work today, I
    can't remember how long ago the futon fucked off & died
Zoology, I'm afraid my father was right to study the behaviour of other species to
    see how silly we are looking at them, or how silly we are ignoring ourselves

I know he is looking for the secret of life, he's just not so self-centred as me
Revealing myself to my doorknob giving me knob a turn

As the door opens & the weather gets absolutely fucking brilliant, testing its
Joints once again, it's a good idea to test your joints before you demonstrate just
    how fucking brilliant you are

Such as it is, I find I am the product of something
Busy with my modes of production, & busy with my modes of

Space Travel

Last night sitting on the bus next to Hazel
who was reading the last 1/4 of *We So Seldom Look
On Love*, travelling ack to Toronto from London Ontario,
I looked away from my own book, *From Next Spring*
& out the window to the north. It was then that I
experienced space travel for the first time.
"Look hon," I said, pointing out the window,
"We're experiencing space travel." Hazel looked
up from her book. It was around nine-thirty
in the evening, the sun had already sunk below
the horizon. All we could see of it was the light
shooting up the edge of the earth into the clouds.
I pointed out how it looked as though we were
hundreds of miles up in the atmosphere, looking
down on a coastline. I thought maybe it looked like
the coast of British Columbia. Hazel wasn't sure
because she had never seen the coastline of
British Columbia. There were islands floating
in a golden sea & there was even a city lighting
up the coastline, certain tiny points of light,
each one undoubtedly the source of a deep & caring
human intelligence. Pretty soon neither of us
could find any trace of it in the sky at all, it had been
replaced indefinitely by another world, not unlike our
own, but coloured by the sadness of what always
seems to be missing from our own lives, the land
& the ocean & the people living in the happiness of those
lights, worlds so dull & predictable the only thing
left for us to do is to make each other happy

in this world with the small precious ways only
we are capable of. Eventually the world in the
sky disappeared as the light outside faded,
so we turned on the lights above our heads
& back to our books, to each other travelling
back to Toronto & our sad but human routines.

Back Seat News

    sit miles
    clouds dot

               if the smooth sky was to blue
               why'd force always

    these trips
    each ways

               its all uphill hear. the grown
               between earth's high diskies

    mountain like
    heavy floaters

               call'd the soons. other landscapes
               growning huge as northern up &

    over head
    winder mined

               as the land's likes by
               the mind's checked out

    ups sets
    north wings

Maybe we weren't so unimaginable as we believed.

A whole race determined to believe in the archives of the soul.
Passion, & that which flies from the mouth cross breath.
Maybe so, yet the emergency of economy never ceases to insist upon a presence.
So how do we, the pond scum beneath the underhand of Those Gods we chose to bypass, push up?
We get so annoyed by the Whole Thing that there isn't much else to do but mildly insist in a kind of slow death by legal toxins & comradery with others who feel the same way.
Such is Toronto in the middle of summer with nothing to do.
Why would we be there deep in the amber glow of afternoons present?
No more.
It is time to begin again, to reach into fall forward & actually catch yourself there.
From another position altogether.
Fantastic to be rewarded with survival, as usual, writing this in the back room of another dungeon-like space.
That's where it happens & it never fails too.
Brilliant to think in this light:

	purge all levels of the floor
TONIGHT:	out the in possible
	mail the list to the page

imaginary tombstones

after john barlow

a dead man walks into a bar. we are all there, all of us, & we all turn to see him die in thru the front door. he walks up to the bar & asks for a serrated blade. they hand him a sack full of narcotics & tell him it's on the house. they do not understand the nature of addiction. no one does. we wonder if he does. he begins to shoot himself in the foot with an imagination gun. it is much better that he be who he must be, rather than us be like him. fortunately, we have all been allowed to remain ourselves. we like it that way, think it's fine, & watch as he dies. it seems like a good idea not to interfere with his project. "after all, someone has to be him on this planet." & he stands for something vaguely reminiscent of what a writer or artist should be in his or her finer moments. but why is there no stopping him? he is dying after all. & we are helping him to remain scared of *them, whoever they are & whoever they happen to be.* too bad no one has bothered to figure out what they really is. it's important, after all, to learn something not only about how we see, but about how the world sees in return. all the directions at once will not bother any of the other harmonics as long as all the parts cannot see their part in the harmonics at large. there is no other, just some reason to think that way. a dead man walks into a bar & orders a coke. they all laugh at him & send him on his way. when he gets there, he's in plain view:

imaginary tombstones

> for john barlow

Life is tedious. Life is boring.
Each day is a mindless repeat of the last.
The people in your life are stupid/uncaring/thoughtless.
Your apartment is a mess. The laundry is
A chore. The dishes are boring. Your cat did
Die. Life is tedious. You are depressed.
Today is the same as yesterday/last week/a year go.
Life tires you out. You are stressed out.
The city is dirty. People die. You are
Angry. You are lonely. Days do
Repeat. Humanity is pointless. Death
Is real. The city is ugly. Life is a
Mindless repeat of the last. Boredom exists.

But no one shall ever come to any harm.

bad days always begin the night before

it will take a while to determine if there's something or nothing
    canadian about that
the next day could be seen as the same as yesterday
it's never quite but just about

seems like I've taken the same route to work for as long as this line
did heraclitus just have another idea
or was it something to reassure us so many years later

uncommon courtesy interrupts boredom
poems like it to present us exactly

so you get caught up one day on everyone else's work but your own
what's better, to be finished
or to scatter everyone's need to see the world unwarped

chant a lonely breakthru at the heart's patched lifestyle
there's always enough time to sometimes maybe

Part Two

SERIOUSLY TAKEN
(2000-2014)

Tree Culture —Some Field Notes[1]

(by Conwenna Stokes)

APPENDAGES: Not the branches, which are part of the body of the tree. Unlike many other species, tree appendages are not directly connected to the body, like the fingers, the breasts, or the penis of mammals. Careful observation revealed that each tree community has its prey and predators, its decomposers and recyclers, its planters and harvesters, its mechanics, its writers, nests, artists, leaves and musicians. These are the appendages of the tree. While they may spend some time physically attached to the tree, for the most part they are in fact entirely separate beings, free to migrate away from the tree itself, like satellites with a chosen place of residence. It is through these living satellites that communication between trees is possible.

ART: Mild gentle brush strokes. Glory.

---

[1] After some study, we decided that these trees were actually more highly developed forms of the local fungus, since they sprouted from the same rich soil that supported all the vegetation of that area. Earlier, we had discovered some particular soil that appeared to be composed of small mushrooms that clung to each other as they struggled to grow out of smaller fungi as they decomposed. The ecosystem was obviously growing and decomposing at the same time in these intricate layers of subtle colours we could not describe. Sometimes we counted as many as seventy-two new growths that managed to sprout from a single decomposition. Other times there were only two or three. Some specimens succeeded in growing as high as our ankles, but it was the trees that were truly magnificent, and it was around their stems that we could find the most interesting samples. When we stood perfectly still we could hear spore pods dropping through the moist air from the spread out canopy of the upper branches. Some round greenish pods we found were the size of tennis balls and we took turns throwing them at one of the thick stems poking up from the ground. They exploded like soap bubbles filled with smoke, the sort we had blown in the schoolyard as adolescents. They

CHILDHOOD: As with every species, the childhood of trees is pure witchcraft.[2] Worship of the sun. Worship of the rain. Worship of the earth, the wind, the clouds. Worship of the grubs, the birds, the squirrels, the chipmunks, the rattlesnakes, the rabbits, the deer, the butterflies, the nuts, the *praying mantis*, the woodpeckers. Worship of the world meditation on fire.

DREAMS: Contrary to popular belief, the dreams of trees are not located beneath the surface of the earth mingled among the roots as a kind of 'ghost tree.' The roots of any species of tree are simply roots, as the earth in which they live is simply earth. The idea of 'hidden dreams' has been a misconception of popular culture for some time now, not only in regard to trees, but with most creatures of the planet. And while having some clever features, such as the metaphor of the 'underground' (ref. Greek mythology) or the subconscious, it is only a limited vision. Once again humans have managed to overlook the obvious. Trees are themselves dreams.[3] We believe this because they obviously communicate in images, as opposed to speech. What they dream of is their own mind and anyone or anything that comes into contact with them. As the leaves of the deciduous are shed during the final months of the year the various dream states of the tree fall away one by one, until the very cen-

---

made a soft popping sound as they exploded in the windless air. When one of these powdery clouds hit the sunlight it created rainbows of deep ambers and purples, drifting slowly through the air until they came to rest quietly upon the brownish leaves scattering that landscape.

[2] Childhood.

[3] Often the dreams of trees will manifest themselves in various appendages, most often in the form of mushrooms and sometimes in the form of flying squirrels. Notice how certain mushrooms are found under certain trees. Their shapes will give you a clue as to what the tree in question may be dreaming about. (This is where we learned it.)

tre of the dream is exposed. Conifers, on the other hand, live entirely masked in a dream, and can never be awakened. It is difficult to view the exact centre of any deciduous tree's dream state, even in winter, when all the leaves have fallen. This is due to the natural masking qualities of snow. Just before the leaves return it is possible to catch a glimpse.

FALLING: It is as though the tree had become wise enough to teach its children a thing or two about mortality.[4] We believe this is why trees are capable of outliving almost every species on the Earth,[5] the only close exception being the great sea turtle.

MIGRATION: (Time Travel via the emotions) Since it is consciousness that gives root to The Tree, migration occurs whenever there is no trace of consciousness present within a three kilometre radius. In the case of such an absence, trees are free to voyage throughout the world by phasing in and out of time upon any available frequencies. This was discovered only recently after careful observation of specific trees grown in a semi-vacuous state. These trees, unable to recognize any forms of consciousness nearby, allowed observers to witness their ghost-like appearance, the mysterious translucence of leaves

---

[4] Fossil records have shown that the influence of so-called academia and institutionalized learning caused trees to have leaves that were as solid as the wood they lived upon. Trees simply had no idea of their own mortality, or cared not to acknowledge it. It was a time in which leaves had no desire to fall, nor did trees have any desire to lose them. Over time, however, with the introduction of human commerce, which began to flourish as early as the Cenozoic Era, trees learned that to ignore their own temporary forms was futile, for it was only their way of living in greed. They were witness to many other life-forms that became extinct, if not rendered completely tedious due to their strange belief in an immorality that they would never conquer. This is why we find such a difference between the skin (constant static) of mammals and the leaves (tempo-immortal consciousness) of modern trees.

shifting in time. Most trees, however, actually fear migration and time travel of any kind, and are much more comfortable in a permanent 'rooted' state. This is the reason why they invite many creatures to actively live their lives in and about them. One should not ignore the species of renegade trees, however, who choose to live in harsh conditions (cold regions, high altitudes, and the like). These are the solitary dream-travellers, who wish for solitude, shifting through the space of time and wind.

PHILOSOPHY: They are your thoughts. Think them. No One Cares. Safety in numbers. Think.

POETRY: As far as can be determined, the poetry of trees contains no known words recognizable in any language of the human race.[6] It has been determined to be quite punctual in nature, but often it is up to any creatures who live within their branches to become their voice. This reveals the humble nature of trees, as anyone who hears this poetry will tend to assume that it is the authors who are reciting it. Trees are in a sense ghost writers of the permanent kind, and wish to remain anonymous, using whatever pseudonyms are available in the surrounding environment. Although it is mostly speculation, the poetry of trees is both open, in a kind of gentle explosive manner, and self-reflective, in a violent implosive manner. This is to say that the poetry of trees moves inwardly and outwardly at the exact same moment, which may also help to explain why trees appear not to move.

---

[5] It has been hypothesized in several well known papers that trees are quite aware of our fate as a species, perhaps more than we realize.

[6] For some examples of tree poems, see the translations we have made that follow these notes.

SEX / SEXUAL PRACTICES: *Each tree is a long slow orgasm of summer*. Deciduous trees are generally more sexually satisfied at the end of the summer months and are therefore too tired to maintain their foliage during the winter months. As long as they have leaves, however, these trees are entirely female. Only after their leaves are shed do they become male. Conifers are therefore female for the entire year, and are constantly in a state of orgasm. Thus the social interaction between trees in most forests is lesbian in nature. One will notice easily, walking casually through a woodlot during the summer, the soft leafy curves and gentle swaying motion of trees bathed in their leaves, as though they were walking sensuously through a dream. One will not notice this during the winter. Because conifers remain female throughout the long winter, this allows for a certain amount of heterosexual interaction during those months. It has been recorded that the temperature in the middle of a mixed forest will always remain a few degrees higher than a forest entirely made up of deciduous, or coniferous trees. However, this does not mean that trees prefer heterosexual activity to lesbianism; it is more that they enjoy a certain amount of variety within the forest. One can also experience the noticeable difference between the atmospheres caused by standing naked in a forest during the middle of summer and rolling naked in the snow of a forest at the height of winter.

SCIENCE: There are no tree scientists. Yet we understand that they are extremely wise and spend most of their lives pondering the nature of their being. When they reach a certain age, they also begin to contemplate the nature of their being as it pertains to those creatures around them. There is a heightened awareness about a mature forest that cannot be denied.

SKIN: Trees are undoubtedly all skin, down to the heart, naked as air. It becomes most noticeable as the leaves, which are not skin at all, but a kind of mental clothing,[7] are shed from the deciduous. This leaves the outer, fragmented layers of their rough skin and genitals exposed for several months. Some species of the coniferous, however, have admitted that their needles are not only a mental sheath, but are an outer sheath of the skin. This allows other creatures of the local environment, even other trees, to live partially, or entirely, within their being for the entire year. We can only assume this enveloping nature is the same for the deciduous, but are fairly positive that this is the case at least for the months of spring and summer. It is strange, however, that despite their apparent shyness, it was the conifers who were willing to offer information about their culture, while the more exhibitionist deciduous declined any such information.

TREE SONGS: Tree songs are almost always songs of prayer. Variations on the word 'wish' usually make up most of the songs and have been heard both in person and from recordings made on hidden tape recorders (example: 'whoosh', 'shush', or 'wiiiith'). To whom or what these songs are directed has yet to be determined.[8] Yet we feel that those who receive such songs are grateful, for it cannot be denied that trees live the most benevolent of lives.[9]

TELEPATHY: (   )

WORK: The work of trees is socio-political in nature, for obvious

---

[7] See 'Appendages'.

[8] There should be more slow noise (music) in the world. Record the sounds of trees for hours.

reasons.[10] Not only do trees live in the community of the forest, but there is also a community of leaves gathered upon each tree. Trees discovered very early that they could live most peacefully in a fourth dimensional system, which is why they evolved as they have. Leaves are all equal and are free to live as they please, while the wooden structure of their trees differ only in size, age, shape, and species, perfectly capable of living their lives as they wish. Each tree of the forest is also free to live as they please, in as much as they maintain their leaves to the best of their ability. The leaves of each tree are in fact eternal to the extent that the tree upon which they exist continues to live. Even though the leaves of deciduous trees fall away throughout the months of autumn, in no way does any leaf die until the entire tree dies, and each one is reincarnated as a leaf in exactly the same place of each branch. This system is essentially the same for conifers, although their leaves, or needles, fall away and are reincarnated throughout the year. It is in this way that the tree can care for each of its leaves equally and fairly, while the leaves may work together for the benefit of the tree, and for any of the tree's many appendages. It has taken trees millions of years to develop this political system, and maintaining it for the benefit of all levels of life is what the tree considers its labour. We are confident that they are doing a fine job of it, simply because individuals cannot help feeling wonderfully easy-going and free when in the presence of such beings.

---

[9] This, of course, is true for the trees of rural landscapes, where our studies took place. It has not been determined whether or not trees living in an urban setting experience the same kind of euphoria. We suspect, however, that a tree's environment has much to do with its state of mind.

[10] Many human utopian political parties have been influenced by trees. See their shifting platforms, available in various fictional forms, for reference.

Trees

(by Conwenna Stokes)

The undeniable, satisfactory crunch
        of the sky through the leaves
                that falls to catch our place,

how I would love to be able to roll
        the words off my tongue
                like branches that go on

forever. The trees say
        our leaves are small and we move our feet
                in times to the winds that sing

too softly for you to hear.
        A Dream in absolute knowledge,
                the very heart of the tree where

no birds sing. They say each bird
        was made to sing its own song,
                different from the others,

and yet the same. They say each branch
        was meant to hold a different bird
                each singing a different song.

Out here my head is as low
                to the ground as a root.
                                  Our breath disappears

with each passing moment,
            a high-pitched wail we do not hear
                                restoring us to consciousness.

Lysdexia in Sunlight

(by Alex Cayce)

what mournful singing
in the happiness of change: they
beat their drums across the cloud-lit skies;

by calling out our names
they are assured of an answer in their wingspan
a note quite high, (not sounded at all within that realm)

something you can hear uttered just in front
of the beak, to layer existence before the sound
itself appears, *a priori*, but so what:

their benign overwhelming attention
can only be explained by
Mind, not by the songs they sing.

Seasonal Drift

(by Alex Cayce)

August contemplation of days, remember to
slow down days again. October... days,
they are, after all, only days; a surface

clouds at three in the afternoon
and a branch that suspends it (thought)
shrink each single motions grows until it

vanish into the perfectly capable blue
(sea monster) (heaven) (wing gust)
but it was the cool rain that came down that

time of year. nice, we thought, to close
down the morning, the evening, and of now.
(the end) to be the darkened skies of

hold the holes of our dreams, all the
excitement, all the lust, now is cool and
heavy (closed) way down here in the

just imagine what behind the clouds

all our little veils falling from the trees
come about their way to catch our little
our thoughts, we are all angels, all

shy birds who watch each of us
clouds out the front room window in
the afternoon, from the inside out

when we remember how we were absolute
(happy) our dreams when they were our
selves, shadows of branches at dawn.

Critique of the Dying

(by H. Azel)

Of the fingers, or
to find itself being meditated upon, great Death
of the day, held or otherwise

these various forms. Sometimes it has
other times it is translucent
but takes its own time to walk up and down

And it grows bored. That fourth
quite rare moment, a shy time
lingers on and sings.

prepare the self for one
mental creature who has opened
two windows, and here are discoveries

designated to be alive at this time.
Building quietly in a green shirt,
what amount of understanding could be

rearing itself in today? Alive,
here to notice that the
not that much different from

will be tomorrow. And I will be
another sky of rare
things retreating in that order.

Something to do will be again in
always disappear

(They may actually change
be content in what I do.)

In Another Shimmering Lifetime

(by H. Azel)

(an attempt at memory for you)
January 1390

I

Picture everyone there loving strangers, met only a few months earlier, their various shapes friendly, filled with chatter. Each of them easily a non-threatening member of an anonymous group of people that did exist once, during the patch-work lifetime of someone who could make their acquaintance and disappear soon enough. In the dark living room, a television flashes dull bluish streaks across bodies and brown bottles; quiet sentences are heard as they pass back and forth between people. Through the doorway to the kitchen a bright land can be seen, where voices climb, and never dare to fall. In that blaze I can see my father sitting around the wooden table with his voice. Those sitting at the table are welcome inside the sound of it, not only as pieces of the discussion, but also as a source for the gentle interplay of mind. A space is present there, where youth has forged a middle-aged being out of challenge and intrigue, a mind that appears to be enjoying his quick rallies, a kind of professing sage, drinking beers like the rest of them, a man who has looked behind himself through those present before him, who has suddenly found himself back at university, this time at the actual pinnacle of a conversation from the vantage point of his own future. My attention is back in the living room where laughter suddenly jumps up and heads for the washroom. Two girls sit cross-legged in front of the television. One of them giggles and a flower blooms from the top of her head, and begins to shine in purples, yellows, and is an attempt to hold all of my attention, but wilts away when the five guys sitting across the couch, each one on their fourth or fifth beer, laugh at a joke about her ass she does not hear. There are others in the room too, figures who are coated in shadow, mysterious beings who at this moment are further away from my mind, ghosts whose voices can be heard warbling over the television like this seven-year-old tape recording of themselves. And the colours there, in that room, grow mouse-like with each stupid gesture, each one a tiny scampering of emotion and fear.

2

Looking into the kitchen my father has vanished.
Outside he is building a bonfire in a snowdrift.
We all crowd to the window, amazed at this, totally our discovery,
and as we admit the novelty of this moment,
we throw on coats and boots and head out in search of light.

Merry once again, finally, and in our drunkenness
we have become wholly unconsciously blind to the ugly possibilities
    of the season.
This is the whole night, what it became in the years to come.
In the future, which is part man, part woman,
there will always be this rage against our darker emotions,
against the cold nature we all come to know as human beings.

A goof-ball escapade of youth trapped forever in the shimmering air,
close to the nostrils and the mouth and the eyes, giving warmth.
This feeling solidified around midnight,
as the soccer match exploded into the empty luminescence of the cornfield
under the mothball light of a full moon; and the girls
choosing to remain huddled near the fire talked about it,
choosing to ignore the drunken shouts of boys
kicking at the black and white ball dad produced from the garage,
aiming each shot between makeshift oil-drum goal posts to the east and
    to the west,
they talked about it in whispers.

On the field there are the sounds of crunching snow and crazy laughter,
they plow into each other for hours, not even keeping score; around the fire
there can be heard the quiet warmth of the first glow,
as it licks at their feet, in praise of the night,

that which knows the soft heady warmth of morning,
and the remembrance of dreams.

And between these places I have travelled in one night,
and at each point that I remained still I was one of the people of
    that place.

(2.5)

(Dad stands near the first talking and grinning,
he is watching the soccer game with his back to the fire,
he will throw on a log or two to keep it going,
the same way he has all night long
throwing matter into our minds for us to use.)

3

And the soccer game was suddenly a stupid ball
caught in a momentum directed either to the east or the west,

without purpose or resolve, finally to stand in someone's footprint marker.
And the fire to which we returned was cheery, but tiring to look at,

and it slowed us down, somehow, and the night grew suddenly lonely and apa
and the heaviness of the air came to sit upon our breath.

And cars began to disappear from the driveway.
And Dad said goodnight and went into the house to bed.

And we had to coax someone from the bushes,
reassuring him that she had not been overly embarrassed by his actions.

And afterward, to let everyone know he was fine, he tackled me,
diving over one of the blue and white oil drums in the dark blur of memory,

knocking the wind out of me for five long minutes.
And the colours of the night began quietly to recede then,

as I lay there near the fire, in the white darkness of the snow.
Feel the teenage rush of it all again receding, under the snowball moon,

a groaning beneath the dark sway of the pines.
And my breath will hang there for all time, like grey angels or tiny stars,

in my mind or the black sky;
there.

Perfectly Ordinary Dream #1620

(August 17, 1925)

(by James Llar)

The imagination could thrive in worse places of the world. It had become this particular newlywed couple's best interest to spend whole days hiding in the most expensive bookstores in town. No one ever bothered them there, and they were free to hug and kiss in the most exciting ways between the shelves. Occasionally they would browse through a poetry volume or two, but they found them dull and vile. They preferred returning to each other's company, perhaps foolishly over a blueberry muffin and apple juice at the snack counter. They were in love at each moment in the bookstore, happy to be holding hands and smiling, ignoring all the literature of the world. On one occasion, they both noticed Edward De Vere standing at one of the shelves, admiring one of his more recently published books. They exchanged a glance of concern. Both were wondering, as young couples might, why such a man would appear in this bookstore. Surely he was entirely out of place. In a room filled with characters dressed in the traditional neon colour'd garments of that country he seemed a parody of history wearing his sixteenth-century wool knickers and vest, the long ruffled Elizabethan coat and a pair of thin black leather shoes. Even his hairstyle added to his ridiculous costume. Somewhat longish, as though he were wearing a wig. It was tied at the back of his head with a velvet ribbon showing the weariness of age. The couple suddenly remembered the five dollars. They began to drift towards the door, shielding their faces as best they could with any available pamphlets, sticks, or newspapers. De Vere spotted them, however, and intercepted them in front of the store. He immediately demanded the return of his five dollars, exclaiming 'How is one to eat if everyone is constantly removing his money from his person!?

A man has to eat, or poetry is nothing!' And he began slapping the young man about the face, though without any real violence, for when one is dealing in magic, violence can only be erotic. Despite this, the young man did in fact find himself growing somewhat annoyed, for De Vere squealed 'Five Dollars!' very loudly in a high-pitched voice for almost half an hour as he continued his assault. In a fit of exasperation, the young man suddenly grabbed Edward De Vere about the waist and lifted him (he was so light, the young man thought) upon his shoulders. And much to the rage and hollering of the great poet, ('Five Dollars! Five Dollars...!') the young man began to spin around and around on the sidewalk in front of the bookstore. The scene is very quiet. It is only the young man and Edward De Vere. No one else dares to enter the picture. At last the constant spinning became too much for the young man, and De Vere was ejected from his shoulders, landing in a crumpled heap in the gutter of the street where he lay for some time, until a smile surfaced on his ragged face. Standing, he straightened his collar (for he wore no tie) gave many thanks to the young man for his hospitality, and bid him good-day.

Perfectly Ordinary Dream #1962

(September 17, 1985)

(by James Llar)

The fall couldn't even wake him up. Luckily,
the movie followed him down...in Slow
Motion. Easiest thing he ever done, ever.
Imagine waking up so deep in the gut, cover'd with
snow from the inside out but finding it warm. Then   [JOHN
imagine not waking up at all. There were so   BERRYMAN...]
many windows in the place when we moved there
it was no wonder that he fell, no wonder he couldn't
revive at that last possible second. And they say if you
die in a dream...
The dull angles of that
particular city were only dull, and grey, though
often bright and tempting at that time of the year.
We knew it as the low motion of Hollywood and
football games what wore them out. I mean everyone,
not just the addicts. We could quite easily live in
this room forever now. This is such a nice view.
Only a little blood on the ankle, sticking out of the
broken windshield. And that's downstairs, it's so
fucking wonderful to follow the angels through an
open window, man, you float about three feet above them
all the way down. Facing the dopey expression
on these poets' faces can only be a parody of the great
literature of the world; it's just a little joke. Just
look at the great literature of the world. And at his hair

rustling in the wind, so vain in its attempt to be the air.
And the stillness of which is the world's greatest
poetry waiting patiently to be discovered.
Then imagine not waking up.

Perfectly Ordinary Dream #4127 (March 30, 1928)

(by James Llar)

The rollerskating was fine, and Ray had the knack, but somehow it just felt like running, nothing special. What he expected to happen and what was actually happening were two polarized events that could occur simultaneously, much like how the past and the future, being only shadows of the present, can occur in a shared moment where neither exists. It was a calculated addiction. Tomorrow, in the bar, she became suicidal, turning up the air conditioner as high as it would go. Several of the customers became white with grief beneath the permafrost, looking like drunken ghosts of people he once knew. She insisted that he drink glass after glass of fine scotch, even though she knew he would only make himself sick. 'I am in the middle of a CRISIS', she exclaimed, and ordered him another drink. Ray wanted to know what was the matter, and in response she ordered him another drink. 'When it comes to poetry', she finally said, 'there is no such thing as time. It is all of time meeting in a bar at the same time.' He decided it was stupid to be there. Meanwhile, in another room of the mansion, Sal was discussing his upcoming wedding with his fiancée Lyllith, his mother-in-law, and Ray. 'The Female Spirit shall surely outlive the male spirit', said Sal. 'And considering how it is that I live, considering how stupid is my life, I don't suppose I can afford this marriage presently. Perhaps at a future time'. And he vanished as quickly as Ray had appeared in the room. Outside, Ray wondered what he had done to deserve this, for it seemed his friend would only propose marriage to young beautiful women in order to tell them about the female spirit. Was he trying to instruct them? he wondered. Was he trying to lure them away from the vacancy of fashion? Ray and his wife laughed long and hard over that one, and he took her hand in his. 'We should call you Man too', he said earnestly. They walked through the snow to their car, each flake falling into that dream in which he had lost the key.

What in the World is Coming to

(by John Elliott)

& we were dreaming of becoming in a world
wracked by misery & desolation, hurt & death.

& we were dreaming of becoming pure energy.

& we were dreaming of becoming love when there
was no love, of becoming hate to fill the void.

& we were dreaming of becoming light.

& we were dreaming of becoming a dream,
dark erotic visitations to each other.

& we were dreaming of becoming root.

& we were dreaming of becoming magic
incantations of a planet bathing us in warmth.

& we were dreaming of becoming warm.

& we were dreaming of becoming
something in the deep beautiful blue.

& we were dreaming of becoming

Fly Agaric (Amanita muscaria)

there is always something
that you know not of, but have
what turns the sense around of it
turns the earth, turns the forest into shade

to sense the solid odour of the colour red
right before your eyes, your eyes
have never, they haven't had the opportunity
to experience such colour, the patience
of an environment, patience so patient
as burning is patient, as violence is

from the centre of the cap there is an outward
glance, one that draws on recognition,
recognition that cuts through the distance of mind,
a projection through time & space
to be enthralled it became everything
everyone wanted the genus to be,
a collective image that somehow flowered
in the realm of the actual world
as though we wanted a part of ourselves
to speak for the entire genus

we have been taken in by the landscape itself
& there is a certain danger in this, although
there have only been two or three cases
of poisoning by this species in N. America
in the past one hundred years

Destroying Angel (Amanita virosa)

hidden, hugged by browns, & held
in the soft white cloud of itself
there under trunk by trunk we stumble up
waiting this way is potential rot
rotting this way is an angel upward

a landing pad for flies & buzz &
thought takes sweat for ether, moist
yur a golden boy up there, moist yur
a golden boy up there, moist yur a
golden boy up there in the s'kid's
kies
      twisted in landing, a parasol
with rosy ochraceous shades at the centre
in the moist & sandy wood of latifoliate trees
waiting is how we will capture the senses
hugged and fraught with non-sense or -being
the calm stature will stare you down,
kick your ass, & leave you for dead
a tight squeeze of illness
constantly in a state of erection
or arousal
the spores happy to be up
down here

luckily it is rare

False Morels

writing operates unless asked to do otherwise
there wouldn't be a chance in hell
a **vice**   two nails   & a faint **shield**:
the nature of a book **dedicated** to its own precision
pits own **desire**. this is a blue poem, the **sunlight** missing
from the world **earlier** than (we) **desire**, & it goes like this:
you wanted to **stretch** my imagination, or at least
suggest that success was safe enough
truth has the opposite view. it is the possibility
of language offered by appearance
in the present that fascinates, a blue blue line
after line out of the shade into yellow
lawning far ahead into the **recession**.
visiting the **paste** every **day** requires decision;
failing to **admit** failure from the beginning.
the **only** way to persist, a green **operation under**
the feather, gonna find me another **home to** understand
this one. for failure **is** a bright sky a black flight
& concrete walk on & wonder back & forth
the city can only **hold** so many still on days **when** the rain
rattles through spring & makes it a **hard** edge to get
around. wait for an **opportunity** then reclaim the treats.
nothing to sell   nothing to hide   the trip
as **is** from the tongue. the **pen** prosthetic **guides**
the work words wear, here, allow me the chance
to see us **everywhere**
they can't see us   they are blind
myopic to say the least.
sealed off from the outside world

communicating indirectly, refusing
to let go of the **remote** control.
between looking & **saying** a division listens
in on this breezing window opens   lifts &
difficult to say, but otherwise we're fine.
they use **small**, handheld instruments, they use
them to **point** their way to **enlightenment**
to raise their bodies above the floor
for a few seconds at a time. this is the **process**
this is the haunting, **edible** & **enjoyed**
but wild should not be eaten **raw**.
every drop of language is stillborn.
no panic through the heavy wait
until it screams a telephone call
i've been waiting for till spring
& **now** that you've found yourself among (us)
you've recalled me to the beginning.
writing operates so far in the air
we only hold it as paper folds to crease
would burn   find time   spit
the foam hard shift from the sideline **demanding**
a politics of **space** hung overhead but happy or
maybe even **another reason** for passion
writing operates **language** contacts.
all that skydigging purely for **effect**.
the four corners of the room
contain affect, defect, effect & **infect**
where you place yourself makes it yet another
four-dimensional model of sacrifice, what you give
given up for something else, comfort perhaps, ease
inoculated as it were by desire blown through the sun.
a ship sails across **nothing**. you look

into the depths of that **nothing**   giving it sound
on bored sometimes you hit **the wires** before noon
bruising the **rest** of a bright after **none** because
how sick are you **of** the words, thinking them up
to death. it churns against the **stomach** happily
inside another version of loneliness. start
making phonecalls to hang up the
switch to letters   open it backward in time.
it rains for five days   having nothing to do
we imagine what it's like to really be alive.
reach for it   **edit** nothing   it happens
all by itself. someone gets up to **read** &
lets us have it. immaculate recordings of local
history scar deep in the greater view
blooming, spreading the word into points
from **each** centre. blues fade to
yellows, yellows to greens shoots a mouth off to spring
from otherwise ink clears the range & spirits
off the roofs in the lane would take notice.
the lengthening days of spring, a casket, this sky
how it gives us the room to breathe a long dream:
a long playing field of some sort & the grass
wet & green dampening the **earth**, soft
underfoot we willed ourselves to the movement of
our long & prosperous days. there is a man, a large figure
in blue, a yellow **necktie**, stands out looking across
everyone watching the ships come in & out of the harbour.
a large man, no one knows he is there.
something about the **clouds**   how they **shoot** off
just **the** right shade over the ocean
such backdrops move too quickly. fascinated
our attention in this writing today is on this man

as he watches cargo   **unloaded**
& loaded from the ships, watches ships come & go
in the harbour, wanting the greater picture of our pictures
uninvolved but watching for hours, watching
trains at railway crossings, counting **each** car, the
hidden meaning to secret patterns tight within us are
discovered remainders uninvolved but at attention
depending on how & where we choose to point the view.
this man is an idea, & it has burst from the planet
in the moment it was given up to the ground.
try to see these plants spiral out of the ground
shoots pushing apart the dead leaves, making way
& it's still raining, the entire shift into the **ear**
where we hear pushed by wind, branches into
the present, writing operates like that
sometimes, ending in the middle to move on
sweep up that cat litter & **dump** it back
in **the** box. keep it clean **say** what's been seen
hear it here & there throughout the **day** i caught
your hair in my **teeth** & held it to **bring** it there.
all problems solved by **lunch** brought to light
as a **feather** a float from the space between us
so we can get down to each other.
a saw buzzes outside **interrupting** the birds yet
again. **rock** doves, sparrows & starlings **returning** again
as **i slide** past on a bicycle wearing **nothing** but
the sound of the crows, murders & murders
to keep me warm. the sound of rain again in the sky
light keeps us cozy keeps us sleepy maybe a little
bored. it's my trucking story so keep your fucking
way **out** of it until there's **nowhere** else for it to **glow**.
technology violates & validates nature, makes it

whatever it might never have thought of writing.
operate nothing.   it's quick.
to fly off the **handle** anyway breaks in the **order**
of things & imagination flexed till broken off
takes time to grow tired of the same old thing.
so i went for a walk. runnymede united church
reaches for the sky that gull is sitting on like a hat
until it takes off. should i notice the grey line against
a great spreading into the hovering air of our
general **concern** for the **living**? you go & tell me now.
take a talk   one foot   at a time.
the flakes **have** fallen but to where in the **end**
is the nature of the game. you were laughing about
something, i said, **here**, & we walked on, down
to **the** low-lying patch of **sidewalk** & **there** it was:
the way out was up through the falling snow
to **land** on any **branch** we could find, become
leaves & melt away just like watching television
with a book in hand   so hard to turn the **pages**
stuck on that same space over & bore into it
under the fingernails until they click against
cups of tea late in the afternoon, the motion of it
of the chairs, moving us closer to the table. **distraction**
always another turn against the cheeky
lust in need of a shave. how this
picks up the milk carton & pours it out
all over the cereal, lets us all grasp **real** action
off the next great movement, **real** shit
the **real** stuff, not just saying but
actually feeling it ooze a way into the
small world of this where there's a place
at the **end** of the **line** in the middle of a sentence

that ends with the first day of spring. so many shit
the first day of spring, go away, go to sleep.
wake up, wake up. go   **live**
right here, in the middle   another walk down
annette with hazel, a look in the byway
at a baby's **clothes, at a** future, at food around
the corner. keep us all together
near the frozen good, all green in a light
built for just an occasion, this **one outside** a round
down jane, a past at shops who never knew
a look into the **falling** snow, a **round** a corner
& into a shop, a one after an other, all along
bloor, **to purchase** around a coloured candle
to buy vegetables, to stop & talk with an andy
for a while outside a green thumb about goings
on of a whatever, & then back **to** a return, to
this **house**, shut the door to settle in, sit down
work some more on the day's writing
pile it on & **colour** it in a little & move on a lot.
you always **have** to move carefully
between things, not on top of them, between things
so dance that **headspace** a mile or **so out**
of your way **right** smack into **the** lake.
swim with the fishes & make it nest, surrounded
by a local idea. i'm the guy **peddling** you
through all this, selling nothing from **one** point
to another, pedalling around & around
always gliding down into gravity
& against it on the way out.
sit still, or imagine it, sitting still
in the side car i'm making through the month
& we'll get **whereever** there is going together

& find out what's doing when we get there soon **enough**.
on the hither side is nothing, something so worthless
it couldn't possibly think it up in **one** sitting, couldn't
possibly think sitting it up in front **of an** audience.
beyond **economy** is beyond mention & that's
where we **should** go **if** we **are** ever to be **saved**
from all the little strings attached.
writing can only do it if we're right here, so pay
attention, it's free after all. what was i saying?
writing operates.   forget it.   now.
what was i saying? nice weather wanders into the room
& hangs about in an open fashion, thinning
space between what hair pours into the skin
widening breath until the sun tells the story
twenty years later. always something ending
into the **midst** of **things**. what was i **saying?**
fuck poetry. fuck it. it mostly sucks, remember
this is what rips out the throat   calling it art.
make live language not language lives.
get in the car & drive away **from it** into **the end**
of the month & **away** from the lettered city, trading
one alphabet for another, then **never**-ending stream
into pooled thoughts **spray-painted** on parked cars.
enjoy watching the words drive away.
too bad we had to miss our ride. a nice sky
over London, Ontario, tonight, high on a hill driving west
& i have to stop to watch the shades suggest
another perfection just that much beyond
whatever **you** tried to say. **it's** all right there.
a photograph of a blue bicycle leans up against a tree.

As Seen from Above

broken down, **each**
note are to per amper
sand the matter. no?
but of the soda pop

break in of the past.
water was a
road cut thru:
a pop in the throat.

landing **on** plastic
they all take off, wait
there, made of several
three hundred years

& top the whole more.
hyporesponsibility
rather than dead.
the form continues.

to arrive in the future
rotate. pick up a
the right mind
a bird stop in mid-air.

you look so unhappy.
tell the bird we left & then
hover. meaning is a bird.
customs, **not** castings

this autodidactic morning
seven species at once.
will they be waiting
under the whole tear

of the light text
for a minute or so?
precision is needed to
feather from further

under the prop, a
bottom, where
as it is pre saint, but
only because. it is a

language. doesn't
anything hanging
trailing the caged
we could get up at

into the sunset? there
wings quick movement
a stupid form, to make
of love **goes**, (goes).

try walking away.
try to watch the world's
important flacks &
vine. this room ain't

unwilling to. another
opens, unwilling to.
an **ecto-plastic** cry of
phone, ring me, a ring

the format can ignore
fascinated by, a fact
i'm **going** away, to walk in
with local species, i will.

nothing else
rooted like this
window for a whole
page. then look it up

As Seen from Below

listen to that **birdsong:**
the note to sea-latter & not

atmosphere. i was thinking
while a clash uv rays to top too

remember coming down. a
horizon between the trees.

the weirdest feeling was
a sparrow, a windchime

& the future the moment
ontario, a huge song

a million notes, long roads
across the species.

ballistic semiotextual
a truck that's broken up

weight **in** the wind.
or is it the room's density

in a certain moron of sunshine?
taoist is always the other hand

busy isming
& looks right at **you.**

to the bird, you want to
go **down** the **street**.

feed to bring in various
anything, **really**, but the

burns in the question mark
once, don't look back.

there, tail feathers tucked, a
story, a motionless narrative

sipped for hours, carved
or slicing at the

dissection the air, to divide
from the next street over.

this a hair in my cup, at the
typo. it's such a nonsense

working at nothing but
so called in a free **exchange**.

that's it. i've never **seen**
off the tail of another breeze.

the **real reeling** of lives.
any moment, just walk.

are **so** many shadows made
here **in** the sight of the wall

one single think, the clever
twitch, & **never** comes back.

point fingers **at** the
position at which nothing.

so simple, of white wine
than the possibility of

compromise, floating in the
swallows **heard** over glass.

we'll get over with the best
looks over the **edge**.

possible? never, more than
lift my head, fill it

always have, no problem
a thing to work with anyway.

we're going to walk into the
page, then look it up **under**

7 Fungal Threads

A

d s
r p
i o
p r
 s e

t m
h e
o m
u o
g r
h y
t

data soft
ring people
it one
people ring
 soft easy

then mutinus
 height easy
one mutinus
 under one
game ring
height   yellowish
then

I

```
   a   i
  w  n  w  s
a  s  e  a
r  a     a  n
e  n     r  e
   e
```


   and in
when   near when slightly
and slightly   edible and
rather and   and near
edible near   rather edible
  edible

J

```
b   r
l t   i
o   h s
o e k
  d   m
      o s
      v t
      e   i
      m   l
      e   l
      n   n
      t   e
              s
                s
```

    brownish   reddish
    latifoliate the   in
    or   however smooth
    or eroded kept
      denomination   more
         or smooth
        variety the
        eroded in
        more   latifoliate
        eroded latifoliate
        now   now
          the   eroded
             smooth
                smooth

L

```
  l
    e
a       n
  (m)  i
n   g
  s
```



```
  lucid
     eccentric
and      near
   (mangin)  in
near    generally
   spores
```

M

```
    s
         p
   (p)      r
 e    (a)     a
     (g)       d
 i              (e)
     n
          g
         s
```

```
   spring
        poplar
    (poplar)    reticulate
expanded    (at)    at
    (glabrous)    decurrent
  it           (e)
     near
          glabrous
            spring
```

R

```
      o
   g  r  h
p  o  a     a  h
i  l  u  n  b  z  o
n  d  m  g  r  e  n
k  e  b     e  o  l  e
   i  n  e  g  w     y
   s  r     r  r  n
   h  e     e     i
         d  y     s
            d           h
         i
         s
         h
      o
      r
         a
            n
               g
                  e
```

            often
          grows   russula   hazelnuts
       purple often   and   and hazelnuts
     in   latifoliate up none becoming zonatus of
     none   dark mild grows russula especially none
        knobby especially becoming   especially often lati-
foliate especially
         in none   especially   grows whitish   yellowish
      stem   russula   russula russula none
     hazelnuts   especially   especially   in
             dark   yellowish   stem
              dark   hazelnuts
            in
           stem
          hazelnuts
        often
          russula
             and
                  none
                       grows
                                  especially

Y

```
h
e   c
 l   u
 l    r
  o    i
   o
          s
  w      i
   h  t
         y
```


```
hand
 edible   can
   lemon    under
    lemon    rusty
     on it
       on
              squamules
   white       it
      hand  thick
            yellow
```

Fact's Mile

'tis upon the point

bites not deep enough
to leave a scar

crack open an anthill
see a human brain
in sunlight

a sound something used
to kill insects
brain stems
and all forms of paper

as clear as 'water' to the 'sky'

unbelievable distractions called
books line up their true weight
think quietly among themselves

who wants the last slice of the log-jam?

something to resemble history
that failed a lot of trees
title pages fixed to stumps

light spring summer sunshine perfume
space wings azure dew and felicity

the ragged edge
exit of sound beneath or outside
a circle of wood

contained in the word *would*

Nearby, Lakes

To get the sense of place a long cool breeze
Rips through the trees the mind and all of that
Can admit that the kid is hungry. But for what?
'Look at the pieces of the sun there,' he says, pointing
To the ground before you, at the wind's dance and
The shadow's etchings, and he laughs, turns, runs
Chews on raisin bread you chew on thoughts meanwhile
To the echoes through the tree's green insistence.
Later you show him bracket fungi on a tree and he
Asks you if they have shells like turtles, and the
Creature is reanimated, renewed, half plant, half
Animal, it now feeds on the slower moving species.
By the casual outpour of words that puts your
Poetry to shame. I mean, the kid's only three.
You can lie to yourself — say you are attempting
To relearn what he does naturally — but know
It is not for you to understand, not even his own
But sometimes, like later, sitting in the middle
Green pieces and the pieces of the sun and the wind
Throws it all through another being's voice, he stops
Looks around, as if to interpret this shift in the weather
As it lifts his head about his face he's wearing green
He says, 'This is real nice.' You make out the words
As accurately as possible. Real. Nice. This is.

Carve

Concrete's not dead, it's just under construction. How I once carved a place for myself in the scene, but now rarely return. Was drawn to the materiality of the word, but lately only words as material. He said it before, the poem being dead, must move beyond the poem. But to what arrival?

Arrival to where I am now, not Kingston, but a language, and a mode of production which requires an outer darkness, and a deeper one inside. Taken with a dram and dedications given to him in his absence. Lick the rim of the brim, and swallow slowly what bitterness has brought.

Replication of past achievements is more of a concern than any assumption that the present is much better than what's gone before. Or that the future promises more laudable returns. Worry that you've wasted a year in your last of the score, and no more progress has been bought with the time allotted. Another notch carved in the knot that you denominate your guts.

Vatic poets are out a job 'cause images have triumphed over the word. And I wanna return to that cave for one more hit of smoke before I call it a night and 250 words logged on the screen.

Eventually this will be lost, like the dream of a concrete poesis that would reawaken the world, make the very stones cry out, or at least make those same stones stonier.

Data

Depending on whether you learn how to read it, the body can tell us what to do. Can bear witness to the vices which have damaged it, can testify to the poisons to which we've subjected it. But to gather that data into a meaningful chart, to map that evidence to reach a conclusion, to break that code of encryption into a readable language, that is the challenge.

To follow the biorhythms ion poetics, to write the linguistic body but to go beyond Olson or even Irigaray. Maybe closer to Herni Chopin, letting the body speak, without the mediation of theory.

To transcribe your dreams into poetry by assuming there is absolutely no latent content.

Home

Once we wrote Home and it was wonderful. Something had come to live in Home, and we thought it was very clever that such a thing could live with us and let us live in Home. Home became us; we became Home. There was a transformation in it — perhaps a reflection of the time we came to write Home. Unnamed creatures appeared as we wrote, living in the cracks and on the shelves and in the corners. They helped us to write Home. Home was a part of our imagination, an imaginary friend, subject to our whims and ideals.

After we had written Home, Home turned from us. What we had written no longer seemed accurate to Home. We looked to the framed painting above the television, but there was no answer. They frowned at us. The walls turned off yellow and mumbled. We could never get the window clean. When we opened the refrigerator, liquid spilled over the floor. When we closed the door, we were not sure what happened. Under the stairs was a strange smell. The hardwood floors yelped at us with each step we took. We have begun to feel Home take on a life of its own, moving away from us: a slow separation of thing and being.

We must write Home again. We must apologize for having originally written Home. We should never have made such assumptions about the creatures that live there with us, that they could remain under our control. Yes, it is time to write Home again, to re-write Home. And I'm sure that it will be necessary to write Home again in the future. By such exercises, perhaps we will come to understand what we meant when we wrote Home.

Privacy

This tree is a speech balloon filled with words. As leaves fall away, the tree becomes less inviting. Craggled old tooth-rot. The more that becomes exposed, the more the tree looks like roots inverted to offer themselves to the sky. Not before the tree's more colourful time, when words are exposed to colder air. As leaves fall away, less and less remains to be said. The less you say, the more you own. The less you write, the more leaves you gather, and the longer you remain cloaked. Shall ownership occur with silence of the mouth or of the typewriter? Take your language to the grave if you have to. Even before you're dead. Let us imagine this paragraph is a tree. What is present gives us language, what is not present makes language useful. There are always things left unsaid. Despicable, foul-mouthed worm. Within you, at the very point words are stripped away. Let us imagine this tree is a paragraph. What is more powerful? The leaves that fall away until you reach the end? Or the roots you never see? What are you trying to hide?

from *The Small Blue*

36. dense joke

how does one get to be like that
filled with excitement
palpitating like an harmonium

steve makes a joke about it
so i start to write about it
the fake fake fake until you die
then steve jokes about me writing

"dense jokes how do you get to be like that"

the lights are programmed to laugh
at "a series of blue postcards"

isn't it interesting
that the poems s/he has written
present a life i cannot believe in

i want to publish a book
by him/her called B U L L S H I T

perhaps all this will disappear
because it all does, and the
voices will go on chattering
to sum the sun

72. drowned notions of passed

real or imagined brilliance of distant classes
calls allow for breakdown of time
stone houses, or of wood, or hours

elements imagine

it looks like hurt, but feels
like stepped stone

how does one write
when people are only interested
in familiarities

things so small you'd
rather not write at all

boredom a relatively recent invention
thanks to the current voltage

the past is so clearly unique
the present gets to become
something that goes on by itself

with me inside it talking about
the most obvious things in the world

rock   paper

    scissors   cobalt

reading about the past
only upsets the small and precious
balance of the present

and have you even
noticed the lack of snow
this winter i mean
it's supposed to be
winter

75. bizarrely tunes itself

they painted in blue figures
to create a foreground and
ruined the landscape

our attention brought forward
without lingering in the distance

it caused me to pick up my canvas
and throw off the audience's
fascination with the obvious

        retreat!

for those whose lament
continues to grow the
vague statement remains

the precious moment:
trillions of stars to the naked eye
a cluster of gas and dust

h.crosby in a tweed suit
with a glass of water
jumps through hoops
and dies precisely

Lack Lyric I

Performances mark the city. Personalities
wait on them for transit.
It is an urban universe.
Small grid of compiled holdings,
thy commerce doth not want
for lack of movement. I
do not care for the
sumptuous caricatures we make of
our architecture. Staring at windows
into our own faces, we

imagine we understand what our
dreams mean. Understand this: the
doors will open upon what
they close upon. All punctuality
aside, I shall meet you
strange sideways glance upon the
advancing arm of the exit
montage. O plans of inner
space, take refuge in the
dark space of the body

take forever to fully comprehend
how light imitates the sun
but is not the sun.
At noon you will simply
fail, and I will ask
my children to prop me
up against my role as

their spiritual leader, or at
least as the guy who
points out the trees. Look —

there's a dead squirrel on
the walk — trade you for
a good theory on language
acquisition. I must warn you
against the purchase of any
more paranoia — stop worrying about
that it's like to be
paranoid glottal stop materialist propaganda.
Let your inhibitions be your
pipe hole to nirvana. Mine

I keep in a small
drawstring of many coloured pornography
to stimulate the seventh and
twelfth vertebrae. Alas, vague structure —
your presence is more than
a curse, it is all.
Yes, all. That's it. Just
all. You want more? Well,
shove off! Go read someone
else's poetry if you need

various poster boy explanations for
the obvious. O clear glass
of water; O very short
skirt. O transparent visual of
repression. I recommend that you
call around to the various

highwire acts banging around in
my papier mâché nightmare of
silicone tarts. Composed from a
position of boredom and restlessness,

today's poetry is all about
what it means to take
bull from the horns, leaving
you shaken, and horny. Between
sense and bafflement, there is
a brief ligature of faith
in humanity that tickles my
sense of bereavement — hours later
exhausted and wanting more, I
turn to you stone cold

to impress upon my senseless
frame a quiet. When will
you begin to haunt me
O smut-ridden hurt of
the city? When will you
remember our cautionary pact to
dull icebox this lidless provocateur?
Hark — a train is coming
into the station — do not
tarry — there is distraction wangling

lightly upon the scene. How,
suddenly, not to be bored?
In certain circles you are
what you write, but me
I am unclear at best.

Perhaps we should refrain from
using consciousness at this time —
it is overrated, after all,
and at best, a quiet
juggernaut of self-destructive military

operations. Just like being eaten
by your very own adult,
the larvae of your mechanical
existence operate the silent cogs;
why can't I just remain
angry and happy in love?
Ah, love, you keep this
city alive, and populated. I
hope you answer my letter
soon. How are the children?

Lack Lyric IV

My two-year-old exclaims
from the next room: 'Aw,
man!' and I know immediately
he shares my passion regarding
NO FUNDING FOR THE ARTS
Yes — he knows it will
be a long and penniless
journey, but he is also
comforted to know that his
nothingness shall be of his

own making and no other's.
And out the door I
go to the money factory
where I slice open pigs
in exchange for paper bits.
I dislike my paper bits
more than you'll ever know —
'and the feeling of them
was most clammy, and without
mirth' quoth the Gray Stone —

'and maybe you'll be lucky
enough to get a poem
out of it, eh? No?
Well, guess I'll go find
some other sucker then.' And
down the road it goes,
a questionable moment of entropy

outlined by a sunny patch
or a queen excluder, something
like a liver fluke progressing.

through the guts of a
sheep. You have to admit,
what feels like an uphill
battle today might bear none
of the effects of the
afterlife tomorrow, and besides,
panic is the perfect tool
to instill a rippling effect
similar to a host establishment.
If I were to relinquish

just one of the twelve
levels of redundancy that naturally
occur, what would happen to
the standards we have come
to understand as support for
such tedious hollows? If you
do not sit still I
will point out your lacks
to the world. And how
strong will you be then

grave digger of this latest
newt report? That is a
lovely sport you're displaying beneath
your left heart patch. No,
not on that side, the
one on the other side,

under the spigot to your
emotional stop-gap. Hmmm. I
wonder what I should talk
about now? Oh, well, you'd

just love that now wouldn't
you. Couldn't you suggest something
that doesn't reflect so soundly
upon your cheeky little sprocket
of profundity and loose change?
These are my days, or
at least what I imagine
of them. And when I
get home my older kid
appears as if by magic.

Where did you come from?
I ask. He demands of
me new toys. He must
learn that what capitalism demands
of him will only in
turn ask something else of
me. I show him my
pig guts, I mean my
small bits of paper, as
if they might hope to

illustrate a certain quasi linguistic
parody of the here and
now. I can tell he
is not impressed. He dons
what he imagines is the

correct mask, but it has
a small debt on it
and this of course makes
me laugh with an undisclosed
amount of charm I later

cash in for a clean
master plan. What a lovely
series of commands you're wearing.
Oh, I'm sorry. I didn't
realize you were another one
of those new multiplication tables
that refuses to give in
to a division of labour.
Man I wish I'd win a
prize and get seriously taken.

Lack Lyric V

Of broken or scarred things:
some love or other is
what we should accomplish. I
guess. And if you happen
to fall may the air
be thin or the ground
be a softer thing than
you imagine. Take this conceptual
sparkplug and close it up
for the night. Tag theory:

You're it. Now you can
chase me down some fascinating
morose umbrage dialectic on toast
mistaken for a mixed green.
Do this or that to
pressure the common fire, take
what we can and move
on through the delicate sunlight's
woven quick kick to the
solar system's dreamy gonad. I

am all that and more,
and so request your love.
Shall it lead me wondering
by the hand to the
assumptions we call home, or
upon an instance slip-free
focus into a moment of

mitosis for all? Face the
facts, darling. Anything you say
is guaranteed to come back

and bite you in the ass.
Good thing I'm going to
die. Good thing you're going
to die. Then everything can
get back to normal. This
is an advertisement for a
few friends. Please drop me
a line — I feel so
lonely depressed filter remnants linger
upon my own sense of

unbelievable circuitry: yes, the circular
gates are wide but wider
still are the gutless wonders
who inhabit this town. When
will I feel I belong
with them? Or they to
me? Probably when my wicked
have been lined up and
shot by my gloomy happiness
fascists. But I suppose when

it's cooked it'll look a
little different. If life is
as existential as all that
why must I put up
with such tedious bullshit all
the time? Everywhere I turn

humans are plastic egocentric fuckers
like me — our demands are
petty, small, and extraordinarily pointless —
dry cough of the six-

-year-old in the next
room goes on and on —
he won't drink a glass
of water to ease my
discomfort. O still thy fingers
O chalkboard of normalcy! Imagine —
there is something wrong with
poetry. I am drinking. I
am drinking. I am drinking
black coffee with withered flowers

and I tell my withered
flowers there is something wrong
with poetry. And they wither
away. So I tell my
withered flowers I have nothing
to say. If the gates
of heaven are simply closed
because they are considered cliché
the weight of my sadness
is more immense than the

efforts some conscious being made
to string words together in
a machine. So shut up
already. Shut up and fuck
me — I need something that

has a little how you
say pizzazz in it. Pretty
soon it'll be years later —
I'll be remembered as the
guy who stuck it to

the man — I'll live in
a pit on the edge of
town where it's quiet and dark
and I can finally think.
I talk with what's left
of my good and eat
meals through a straw. Each
weekend I'm visited by my
feelings. During the week I
type poems on their behalf.

from esp: *Accumulation Sonnets*

forlorn falls of autumn
the light shrinks to whole
itself the size of night
putting the shape
of letters into each size
as an equation meaning
respectively speaks for
this moment or that one
trades black for blues
pens' commercialism
'the true value' a line
on this inside out there
the family a group of
different sizes to acknowledge
the passage of one's age

oh so this is your sidewalk
the software of weather
so mysterious to clouds
i don't know about you people
or machines of the overcoat
i would like to transcribe the rain
hear an elegant example
of extortion personified
suspects fall for december
the year the eyes fell open
against winter and cried for pulp
there is some abstraction going on
deep in aspic of language
this wet city wants words
meticulous or some other

the bits of light that don't repeat
the notes off keys
sky cabin fever a buzz
or burn of scotch
tape sounds or stereo
phonic purr of soft slurred ice
something to call memory
presents gifts beyond things
figmented techniques between
sounds like between to me
artificial followers and
breeding whirlwinds for energy
we require caffeine at least
i do anyway green caterpillar
a pure state of floor once at all

the sun goes down how narrative
operates daily aliens devour the boy
poured out his drink all over the book
i was reading not paying attention
to him a belief i have that poetry
happens small and in spaces between
people and the failures of language
we are alive in and i have a son
who can be an asshole at times
like me i rage with him about
a book another book in a series
of meaningless objects we are forced
to live with now i can read it in
the tub and nothing will ever fall
far from the tree at all

star covered seams of church daze
slots or bicameral blindness looking at 'at'
where there was a word i erased there
enter stage fraught the solid imagination
of leather games and piddly winks
jammed hands in the disabled
click of boot heels into the sun
set the words straight again
or at least align the line
'insert three lines to obscure'
the fact three lines were removed
for aesthetic and or personal reasons
space for the solid image of reason
in the life of contemplation a thought
more like architecture than space

skim elk clop soda
fir or balsam or pine
sun and shade and cold across
a birth that starts time
these explorations of monotonous
mouths or words like hallelujah
stain glass that speaks and says
these days deep thought is cheap
but all we have to compare to in
finite principles or the inner
edges of the boards stamped
with gilt as charged in cloth
recall a lovely day of snow here
a monastery of the mind
falling so quietly from the sky

in the future manifesto
the right now sun is awk
words rattle sprak rather
cloud cover silly guitar
drum and whistle combo
occasional pirated suffragette
to the sound is water
couldn't we be twenty-five
in a rock band some
balance beam could imagine
the stick knifed in
or eggs of avant ages
this species of cattail
handle or zeros i'll hanker
a leaf about the root

Lake Ontario Suite

I

Blue shape of the lake to the south:
who says morning is not the source of our faith?

Eyes open. Splotches of sunlight and green,
air through the trees, movement of thought.

Thirty-three years old and I still don't understand my place.
Here the sky calls, a bird hovering, the edge of the wind.

The baby sleeps; white birch bend in a green season.
The imagination of Lake Ontario broods nearby:

deep creatures rise to float in shallow waves along the shore,
wait to be pulled back down. Even the dead things — no one will wish

anything on them. Shall they weather the stamina of what we know?
Lightness and dark, the visible spectrum, difficult variations.

What must lie in their form, or simply cease to exist.
Either way, it's only natural.

II

We walk along the cliff a safe
distance from the edge. The
rough water after a night
of rain, the solid earth soaked
through. The boy runs ahead,
his hair caught in the sun
disappears into lengths of green
choking the path. I hold
the baby. He yawns, points
at some ships, and is satisfied.
Our children: the ones we
let go of, the ones who let us
hold them to us. Such ambiguity —
a mythology of what we create
but have no control over.
Hair reflecting the sun can
be a code of unintentional
vagueness: it scatters insects, pollen,
a bird who squawks at the
air. The baby points, understands
his connection to things that
move. And if they do
not move he must move
them. I wonder when this height
will fall away into the lake —
how can we measure erosion
if we will not bear witness?

A snail clings to the
stem of its small universe,
the source of its faith.

III

So many undecided secrets:
the desire to be left alone

and the desire to participate:
two sides of the same un-tossed coin

leave it alone:
the full moon over the lake at night hangs there

nothing more:
a vague harmony

déjà vu among the living:
miles and miles of water and land

between them the shore:
malleable space

link what moves unceasingly and the immoveable:
where things happen

we do not walk too close to the edge:
lessons in mortality

IV

The boy returns, wants
to know what dead means.
Asks if the dead fish down
there will come back to life
and swim away. Will he
come to his own conclusion
if I do not answer? The
stink water strikes below the
cliff again and again. The
fish floats in it, white,
bloated, a thing larger than
I thought possible from
brooding Lake Ontario.

We walk on. Think quietly.
Picture full moons over the lake.

On Vocal Technique

Immediately behind the back
Back behind the rear posterior limbs
There are two wide semicircular plates
Plates wide as the open roads that
Circle and slightly overlap one another
Overlap and then overlap another of
The right-hand plates as it lies
Over the right-hand plate lying over
The left-hand plate. These are the shutters —
The shutters, the lids, and the dampers
And together they dampen
The sound of the musical box.
Let us remove them. It is a technique
Of borrowing the membrane of a film.
The music, what the poet once said
To the right and to the left
On the right and on the left
Inside where lie two spacious cavities
Wide spacious cavities, we
Shall say they are wide and they are
Known throughout the provinces
As the chapels. Together — together
With the poet and what the poet said,
Together they form the church.
Their forward limit is formed
Limited by a dry membrane
Coloured like a soap bubble
And known to the poet as the film
Upon the mirror of what the poet said.

The church and the mirrors
Reflect and the dampers reflecting
The various sightings of the person
(Not the poet) — these are commonly
Regarded as organs which together
Produce the cry. Of a singer out of breath
Using breath one says that she has broken
Her mirrors. This is followed by
A moment of reflection. Meanwhile,
In another reflection altogether
The same phrase is used as
The same phrase a poet once used
Without inspiration. Acoustics
Abound but lie flat, the song is lacking,
Can you hear it? That acoustically
They have given in to how
Their lie reflects popular beliefs.
You may break these mirrors,
Shatter the song and the sound
Of what the poet said, but not the
Poet. The poet, the mechanism
Of the poet, does not exist.
You may remove the covers
With a snip of the scissors
Heard resoundingly as the echo
That tears across the yellow anterior
Repetition of the membrane, but these
Mutilations do not silence the song
Repeating the membrane of the phrase
The poet has not yet begun to speak
The poet does not even know she exists
She only knows that poetry exists

And the membrane dampens the sound
Merely changes its quality to another
Quality and weakens it until finally
You can make out the voice
As it reflects upon the sound:

> *The chapels are like poets;*
> > *they do not produce a sound,*
> *they merely reinforce it by*
> > *the vibration of their anterior*
> *and posterior membranes;*
> > *the sound is modified*
> *by the dampers as they are*
> > *opened more or less widely.*

Thus it is spoken. But the actual
Source of the sound is elsewhere,
The acoustics are obvious and yet
As sound become somewhat difficult
For a novice to find. To find these
On the outer wall of either chapel,
Hill, or document, look approximately
At the location of the ridge formed
By the junction of back and belly,
Overlaid with tiny reproductions of
Backward sounds and glances, and
Find a tiny aperture with a horny
Circumference masked by the horns
Of the quiet overlapping damper
Overlapping the damper. We should call
Out: This is the window! This opening
Gives access to a cavity! Or

A sound chamber! Deeper than the
Chapels! Or a Poet! Oh, but to be like
This much smaller capacity, this chapel
Inside the smaller chapel. Inside
Is a poet. Immediately behind the poet
Behind the attachment of the
Posterior wings behind the attachment
Is a slight protuberance, an almost
Egg-shaped protrusion, which is
Distinguishable as an indistinguishable
Extension on account of its
Dull black colour, a colour taken
From the neighbouring integuments
From which it takes its colour
And are covered with a silvery down.
This protuberance is the outer wall
On the outside of the sound chamber
That calls out with the sound
Of which we speak. Let us cut it
Boldly away. No more shall it
Remain uncut or unspoken, we shall
Lay bare the mechanism that
Produces the mechanism of
The sound, but not the sound itself,
The cymbal of sound. This is a small,
Dry, white cymbal we shall call a
Membrane, oval in shape, convex on the
Outer side, and crossed along by its larger
Diameter is a bundle of crossed
Three or four brown nervures
Which gives it elasticity and the
Technique by which we may

Describe the mechanism. Its entire
Circumference is rigidly fixed.
Let us suppose that this convex
Shaped scale is pulled out of shape
From the interior, so supposedly
That the shape is slightly flattened
And so quickly flattened and
As quickly is released; it will
Immediately regain its originality
A voice of such convexity
Supposedly owing to the elasticity
Of the nervures which are pulled and
So quickly flattened and as quickly
From this oscillation a supposed ticking
Sound will result, the result of which
If you are hearing correctly, is the
Supposed sound of which I speak, the
Voice, the voice that has been speaking,
The voice of the poet speaking.
And to think that twenty years ago
All Paris was buying a silly toy, called,
I think, The Cricket!

Woods Pages

I

How to desire that crackle trees half
empty of leaves crackle? A mind that
will run their minimalist instincts
through an environment only to
build nests in the whole of the sky. So
ghostly I recall some talk about
their presence, like names for mammals,
truncated communication that
listens carefully to the dispersed.
To listen to the wind is to see
a love, the feeling of settling love.

II

Autumn: some landscape the edges of the skies pulled
toward the earth for leaves to kick up the wind.

Can you sense the moment leaves halt for a fleeting
distraction of silence? Walking listens aloud

for the sound. What all the nameless creatures name. Some
relationship between two species in which one

obtains nutrients from the bodily functions
of the other. Or could you possibly hear how

long the walk to chorus-less songs the lingual tics
are as likely as any to empty into.

III

Out from under
the foliage scoots
a leaf scream. Through
the last relief
another small
season lives, not
as a voice or
the tethered sounds
of the ether,
but the hours a
memory hangs
in an autumn
morning itself.

IV

A memory called late October
slows down the days around the so-called
point. Regard the rotten tree-falls such
and such waits under. Ah, toe nudge. Your
gentle words fall, and will never see up
again. Cool fungi, go on: feed from
the dead. Walk across the air to the
next wood. Perhaps these woods are tied to
a hook of letters invisible
to the naked enjambment of our
lives — and the trajectories mammals
insects and birds weave into a land
to give it an immediate sense
of failure we learn to call decay.

V

Is it merely decay? Or is it just writing?
Small possibilities in a sensual act, how

sculpted could a grotesque change in the future be?
Is a culture of failure a happy culture?

Anyway, who needs more than a canopy needs
to those accumulation drinks of from the sky.

Leaves follow to the sound of shoots, the daft process
of germination weather unseasonably

flows out of, and the despair of knowing where to
go without thinking about it goes on breathing.

VI

A leaf. As breath
continues what
sound could it make
to satisfy
the quiet of
the realm? If it
were another's
dream of such un-
manageable
germination,
the voice might roll
over the land.
It continues.
Do you hear it?
If you did could
the land settle
for sweet breezes?
If it did would
you be special?

VII

Only as meaningful and only
so when the senses have been blown through
an acorn the size of a human
brain. Silence is the only theory
a seed to the ear reveals. The sound
doesn't play in a shell's ocean, but
in the wind. Of the pauses held against
contours in a sky the grey matter
makes of itself. A receptacle
as spectacle: a moment of self.

VIII

Patient for lines, impatient language asks of trees
who has spoken lately? Who has shed their leaves in

this long tradition of the best of the worst to
become the long arm the world casts out: great shadows

deliberately tedious, meticulously
limitless? I must ask who draws which attention

from who. Who owns the woods when the owls start to call
themselves a play on words: that first hoot a hollow

the second fills in for the third's sheer panic. The
wind dies away. Warm softness. Imagine the sound.

IX

Could you be lost
in the midst of
such a view? Shall
we record what
creeps in upon
our emotions?
The owl's desperate
eyes continue
to hunt for high
sundown in their
prey's flight. Witness
the bulky
dissection of
panic from the
occasional
rustle. At day's
end such huge brown
leaves take off to
hunt throughout the
imagined snow.

X

Later than we thought of what it was,
where dreams of the missing sun inside
the knots of earth protrude, we looked to
fortify the basic wooden land.
But the verdant always supercedes —
will supercede you. More than brown or
green or grey or all the shades therein
the wind is rewound with certainty
until you can smell the rain. It was
an idea we had. After blue
there is nothing: no lines, no nothing.
No chiselled work as though from one stone or
wood. This comes to mind as I emerge.

XI

What suggests the call of the woodpecker is an
engraving? Listen to it hollow out the air.

It calls to you. Or at least you imagine it
does, and somehow are unsatisfied in becoming

drawn through the puzzle. Metaphysical in so
far as the details are maintained as such; details

to suggest the ninth quote from the second book of
miscellany is an arbitrary hybrid

constructed by language. What is there to hold on
to? I have this very fine edge of the world: sound.

XII

Tell me the call
of the crow is
rooted. Tell me
to build in the
heliotropes'
reversal of
silence. The bird
calls lead all too
quickly, and
without warning,
to the parting
of this first sound.

Lift

Today it's the horizon you're wearing
Around the ankles, a blasé fortune
The island drips as a mortal sort of scaffolding
Wearing features lightly upon an owl a crushing weight
And I am sitting in the back room ruminating

And outside the window I am looking through
Is a bird singing and hopping around in the lilac bush
We planted so many years ago, a bush that's been
Growing now as long as we've been living here and that
Fornicates a scent so mysterious and alluding it invades
Our lives so friendlily each June it just pains me
With an unspeakable rainstorm of fear to realize
We will leave it behind when we finally move away.
Poor little tree! What is it about empty houses,
Or at least the possibilities an empty house
Proposes even if it isn't empty

At the same time I'm wondering what the precise
Name of that bird is, not the names that I'd give it
Such as *The Small Brown or Black or Grey*
I Can't Quite Tell Because of the Hiding Among
The Leaves Bird, or *The Ontario Catfood* but
The actual precise accepted name
And this is when you enter the room
And you are wearing the horizon around your
Ankles and you tell me it's a tit-mouse

The Lyrics to Your Next Hit Single

Take care, song, that what the stars imprint you mirror
in a minor key — they are neither subject nor object
conspiring distant harmonies among the ignorant.
Perhaps one day there will be millions and millions of them
strewn all the way through your ruins, with no moments that will lose
sight of what hears the sound of the lakewater. Dreams congeal
into perfect shade, grown perfectly, so shy in the
white moon-rise on the meadow, whiter than clover.
In the midst of such an immense, soundless, and high concern
the shattered rose of insomnia barfs softly
upon the tax of deathless vulgarity, a quiet spasm of grit,
feeble and cold on the horizon. And so,
blessed are the dead. Oh dear dead that the rain rains upon,
nightly under the simple stars decomposition poses
for what all the cameras have left behind:
something with clouds for shift marks as if it makes a difference
without the power that makes less hard.
Today your genes want to live!
They are made sharp by air made sharper by their smell,
the technology of luna moth, and the words "how to love."
The jar that refused to go dry at the end of the day
surprises the value of every single object
with all the misery of manila folders and the mucilage
parked for so many years on a side street with unlit lamps.
Eventually the slope gripped at their feelings
with the sudden wrinkle that solemnly declares:
"what shit war is" — then pauses for the commercial break.
No picture has been made to endure this, nor will it live with
the little box that remembers her childhood.

It is like the ground, like a part of the ground, a modification of the ground
an awareness that metaphysics is a consequence of not feeling very well.
Do you hear your footsteps in the next room?
They are as a sea will be like the fire, a blaze of heat,
wax drops on a dress
under the influence of some sort of water vapour
growing out of the photo of the two of us growing old.
Our flowers yearn for the tenderness of silent winds
in some vague task beyond the window glass
with your studious incursions toward the pomposity of ants.
My dear photographer of the sky, snap on!
And afterwards perhaps you'll begin to comprehend dimly
the sorrow for the loss of that which we never possessed.
Residing in the submerged shafts of the
tracks that lead through the pools of dead water
are the materials changed forever into an abstract crystal.
And suddenly a hare ran across the road.
Are these the words that passed, their pain discarded, cut away —
here I feel I should explain the contradiction of waves,
the creeds of difference and the contradictions that are
like metal poured at the close of a proletarian novel,
sweaty with a secret dark, crummy with ant-stale,
their dark unsilvered treetops etched across the sky
as though the earth had a saint's image tattooed on her belly.
They shun you though you're the one feeding them,
and they grow blacker upon the soundless, ungurgling flood
of your huge and birdless silence. In their wake the growth
may hide another emptiness. So pause to let the first one pass.
The beautiful ordinary light of the patio is like
a hand that draws nothing except the
peace we have to die in. Dense green laurel and grim cliff,
let me come with these donkeys into your land

to follow in your tracks on the high road. And if that eye is not a cloud,
the weather is motionless, like this cold skirting along the hills —
this is the refuge of the artists, full of mirrors, musical instruments, and pictures,
and ghosts from the ovens, sifting through crisp air
to give the knockout lick to your bad luck
in an airy defiance of nature.
In this shadowy silent distance grew the Iceberg
death, but by drowning on an inland sea
the trees add shade to shade. The lights are out in the houses,
now we'll both be lonely
with bent shoulders, mixing the thread on our fingers
with sleep. The log that shifted with a jolt
is as high as can be, with the blue bunch of grapes that flares and celebrates
arms that are braceleted and white and bare
as if men were birds flying up from their own swamp
so ignorant of any weather not their own.
And wood and wood-bank shall enchant us onward.
There are so many things a man sees at the precise moment
of the middle of his life,
yet how much room for memory there is
down within these galleries of sheen, of flux.
And the autumn sigh of starlings
shivers through transparent cities mounted on yaks,
caught in this stillborn dog in honey.
A man lives in such a house. He plays with the serpents he writes
as everyone goes home so lost in thought.
Soon I will know who I am.
I will play the deadly game of chess with this book held up like a mask,
and different pairs of hands will speak
as though the game was fair. The moves one makes
lashes the other with shadows that hide beneath my lids
and teach free men how to praise their own

unquestioned facts with a record of pebbles along the way.
To those who want to give themselves vast strange domains
where adoring woolly-haired natives proclaim
down with those who count out their tomorrows:
from everything a little will remain
through air or vacuum, snow or shale, squid or wolf, rose or lichen.
We arranged our lives in the flowerbeds and the shadows,
in one rainstorm after another, and will remain
upon the reflection in someone else's mirror.

More Trouble with the Obvious

The kids are busy
with objects they find
at their disposal but
they use them
all otherwise —
a stick is a gun,
a shoe is a gun,
a wagon is a gun,
the chalk drawings are guns,
a used piece of chewing gum is a bullet,
a round smooth stone is a crown —
they haven't noticed how the wind
shifts the leaves in the trees
the same way it shifts their shadows,
not *exactly*, but it's okay,
I wouldn't be able to explain it anyway.
Isn't it wonderful the way they play
We Will We Will ROCK YOU
over and over on their little toy pianos?
Then they turn them into guns
and blow you away.

Timely Irreverence

The snow outside.
White that makes things
taller. The fence, for instance,
or the branches of the trees,
all their lines layered now beneath
lines that seem thicker than their weight.
I'm inside. I'm tinkering with these lines
while I wait patiently for the hippies
to die. When that finally happens
a great weight will be lifted
from our shoulders, and
we will, at last, be free.

Part Three
New Poems (2014-18)

On Time

For this next poem you will want to
imagine that you are a human being
who is reading this poem, caught
precisely between a moment of
experience and one of action. What
will this action be? Whatever it is it
won't be some meta moment you
will come to envision as the result of
reading the poem, because the poem
hasn't happened yet. And when it
does you will have an actual
experience, something that is
happening exactly in that moment.
Our time on this planet shapes our
understanding of time itself. If one
breaks character — the spot you are
standing on — the anticipation will
be lost and the world made a little
less hopeful. You will want to be
prepared for that. Meanwhile, try to
resist the calm eroticism of your
smartphone, which you will surely
be drawn to as you wait for this
poem to begin — it will be
difficult to resist because you are
unconsciously aware somehow that
the poem you are about to hear was
written, at least in part, on an iPhone
by a poet who was unable to pull

away from the calm eroticism of touching a screen during a moment of composure that occurred while listening to a reading about the science of sleep. But you have greater resistance than the author of the poem you are about to hear. You resist. You are patient. You have been built to listen. And in the next poem there will be thoughtfulness and politic, beauty and rage, and you know this. In fact, you have the distinct feeling that you already know the fate of the poem you are about to hear; it is the same feeling you have in general that you already know the fate of the planet — everything has been dictated somehow by the brave enormity of the past and the evidence that has been laid out before you in the present. And regardless of your own imagined destiny for the poem or the planet, you are fairly confident that you will outlive the reading of the poem you are about to hear while at the same time you are positive that the planet will outlive you as it recites its long mournful notes orated in frequencies beyond what any living creature can hear, let alone comprehend. You and this next

poem have a lot in common, you
decide, as you wait patiently to hear
it speak to you, you sweet, sweet
human face.

Gathered for the Purpose

Overlooking Georgian Bay
tiny edges of waves white
against deep water — this is
an experiment in intimacy

and I won't ever die just yet.
Foot after foot atmospheric
melodies repair each tone
higher than the next, a trail

of geographic outcroppings
& visual stimuli that oppose
news. What sit there remain —
millennial drones of rock

& shoreline collections of
mosquito bites, a pure pure
Canadian tropism entered into
the record books as whims.

Do what you must do:
identify the master in all things.
Deep in the rooted projection
of these trees, words are

miniature shadows awash
in biological features that have
driven out of the city. When
you need them to step out

from behind layers of electronic
vulnerability & speak, they do:
"tiny edges of waves white
against deep water." It felt

like a good place to stop.

Conceptual Poetry

That's when you pulled
out the Sapphic quartet —
reminisced bitterly on the
subject of women who
reverse their direction
seasonally in response
to root systems.

'It's fine' is what you
said, finally taking up
the harp of your father
'I can harvest emoticons
for their personal value.'

Yet the whales drone on
for pleasure amends history.
You'll learn — functioning
badly in a large dream
is an even larger
version of time travel,
a marvelous application.

Slower than oceans, less
firm than nouns, deep
in whose depths great
mammals display the sonorous
we-shall-inherit-the-
earth melodies that deny

you wait. One day
you'll feel the holes.

A Sentient Being Rises from the Sea

There's nothing but a circle
to charm an island into
believing that it can see
myself as part of circular.
And the sky is a
blithering sequence of nonsense, but
it's still the sky. Isn't

it? So what can I
do but plan ahead, to
create that place where we
both exist civilly, where we
can carry on together without
worrying about what I is,

or what we could become?
Somehow the world always asks
us to stare it down —
but we don't — that would
be too simple, some other

reason to bleed out rather
than evaporate. And we have
no medical insurance. Every night
I turn out the light

in that room across the
hall, or is it the
light in your eyes? It's

hard to tell. They both
shine. But either way it's

always the me that disappears.

The Shiny Things

to the memory of Barbara Godard

I AM A MAN OF CONSTANT SORROW

In the early days the Hospital, with a bed capacity of sixty-four, provided only eight private and two semi-private rooms.

A GIFT

This sketch is unique in one regard, as it gives the blockhouse at the east side of the Windmill. It is the only drawing extant which shows the old fortification.

EIGHT SQUARES

Generation after generation of its people have brought it from clearing to town, from town to city, from city to metropolis.

SOMETHING'S HAPPENING HERE

With refreshments wine was usually served and sometimes stronger beverages, and it was not an uncommon sight to see men reeling through the streets and sometimes uproariously drunk at the close of the day.

DEADLY VISIBLE RAYS

In the late thirties there was some discussion relative to the introduction of gas.

THE WORLD TODAY

Let's recall here that we're talking about someone who states flatly that he arrived on Earth from space in order to save humanity and bring harmony to the world.

THE AFTERLIFE

I also stated, that the navigation was not impractical in itself, but from our ignorance of its course; and that our late experience would enable us to pursue our voyage with greater security.

THE MODERN CRISIS

In very early times a herd of these tremendous animals came to Big Bone Licks, eating all the grass of the countryside, and beginning the universal destructions of the bears, elks, deer, buffalo, and other animals which had been created for the use of man.

SYMBOLISM

The critique is remarkably contemporary: imperialism is criticized for having no regard for difference.

A MESSAGE FROM THE LOVED ONE

But what is certain is that his special take on the master narratives of freedom struggles remind us that much too often they wipe out embarrassing realities whose memories might make us less self-righteous.

A PROVERB

The narrator, as a white male, is expected to be completely voiceless in a liberal world.

THE TERRORS OF PUBERTY

Is that a turkey or is it a baby or what is it?

THE DOORS OF PERCEPTION

The English, too, could show lack of fairmindedness at times.

THE PENNILESS WIDOW

Canadian history is dead. Long live Canadian history!

SPRING RETURNS

If it cannot be explained in "rational" instrumental terms, then it cannot be explained at all; violent women must be either trying to be men or just crazy.

BAD NEWS

For example, when Canada figures in the American imaginary as a northern "beyond," or fails to register even as an *absence,* much is already being stated about the relationships of power between the two countries.

MASSACRED BY THE INDIANS

To her relief, the conversation turns to the subject of ocean currents, about which Steve appears to know all there is to know, and to the tiny beings, tons of them to the square mile, whose life consists in being swept in serene fashion through these icy waters, eating and being eaten, multiplying and dying, ignored by history.

DEATH IN THE AFTERNOON

This literary transference of male war imagery to female love poetry is one further sign of her literary ability.

DEATH BY DROWNING

One was behind the armchair, between the window and the door; and in the corner beside it, on a little wooden bracket, was a tiny statue of Hercules a few inches high in old discoloured marble.

SUNBURN

The wonder is not that so many of us fail, but that so many of us succeed — that we aren't all walk-around, wind-up children, sexual pygmies for life.

CANCER

There has developed a dramatic contrast in the relationship of the working class to the process of production and to that of consumption.

MALNUTRITION

Neither the possible static nor the volume or the particular station affects the fats that the radio is *on.*

AN ORPHAN LEARNS TO COUNT

The proposal seems to confuse the dietary management of disease with the establishment of monotheistic authority.

MY BEST FRIEND

That scrap of shriveled leather, that wasting impalpable bulk of feathery print, was his Bible; there lay the medicine chest and there the sewing-machine; and this, this intricate ruin of molten metal tubes, charred rubber, and dislocated machinery, was the harmonium, its scorched ivory keys strewed round about it like teeth fallen from a monstrous head.

PATRIOTISM

Violent scenes. Jealousy. Reproaches. The men fought, decided that the friendship of men outweighed the love of women, clasped hands, drank together for the whole of a night, fell together into a canal together at dawn...all according to the book.

THE PROBLEM OF EVIL

Between chilling howls and shrieks, the car kept moving, until suddenly, without warning, it left the darkness of the tunnel and jerked to a halt in the bright light where the ride had begun.

MY NAME

The look from the person at the front of the room,

a left hand caging a left eye, communicates that it's already too late, that we are already sitting in positions strange to this endeavour.

The Nature

These imitations of time
cramp my style. Here, this
is a window. It's just for you.
Inside is a room. The
room is vast. The vast is
becoming. Look! I'm
actually foaming beautiful
colour into my hair! Please —
let me sell you something.
My hair is my head and the
rainbow is a protest song.
The song trickles along a
geography of what we have
taken the time to learn enough
of to retrieve "it." I am not
embarrassed, I am not
anything. And yet, in
retrospect, there is no
looking back, for we are a
culture of beggars who
look forward. So here we
are in the space time travels
in and I am unsure of the
future. Is it where we should
really be heading? Should
we rely on the great flattening
of the world? Every day
the quiet revolutions of
the masses make way for

the most useless of poems.
And by poems I mean
human beings held aloft in
the grid of their various
inventions. Their inventions
ignore the dead and the
weight of uselessness that
has been given to us all. Dear
dead poets, unite! Don't be
forgotten; don't let the world
shove aside your little poems;
don't let this poem lose
momentum — a confession
out of the blue: I have never
been brave enough to simply
confess, and if I was there
wouldn't be much to tell.
I admit it, your confessions are
far more advanced and the future
is far more with it than this poem.
Average stuff, thoughts atune
to the physical limits of
my own attention

Our Journey from Silence

Somewhere there is a space between us —
the stars are so far away and yet they float
as tenable occupants; enough said. Forget the
stars. What I want to say is that space is
overrated. Even stars get to sit in it —
space — ha! Forget space. How different is
that from us? There comes a point in every
person's life when *it* becomes impossible
to negotiate, but only because you suddenly
realize that life has stopped giving you
things and has started taking things away
instead. So, what to say about this place
now? It's full of people, all waiting. Some
wait for people to die some wait for
people to heal all of us are waiting for
our indemnification tags. If you take a
room with no windows they give you $600
back, but I'm wondering if I can just go
on holiday with my Game Boy. I keep
forgetting that humans are frames from
which genitals have been hung by someone
with an evolutionary sense of humour.
Ha ha ha ha ha ha ha ha ha ha ha ha!
So it seems reasonable for a mildly attacking
timely semi-precious untoward sky,
or any other imagined phenom of nature
I can dream up, to be that something we
might use to flick the puck against and
blossom noise germs. When you read

this, my biographer, you will know what it
is like to rise quietly out of a culture of hacks
hacking on the debris of their genetic ancestors
that make up the culture they claim to excess.
No, that's not a rubber grouper I'm holding in
the author photo, that's a pigforker. And now,
after years of working on this, I've discovered
that if you are going to insist on using the
vocabulary of the masses to write I am going
to have to insist that you hang out in the
depths of space like a star.

Another Poem About Time Written at the Onset of Middle Age

Now that nothing is for sure and everything is stable
I no longer have the words to tell you that one of
the loveliest things is that time passes.

Other than a vague noun for something that has
been there all along, what are some words for time?
Time is a form of sensibility.
Kant said that. Kant also said that
space is a form of sensibility, but
there is a distinction between that sensibility
and the sensibility known as time.
One is successive and one coexistent.

But do you really care what Kant said?
His relationship with time is over, and as for space
Kant passed through far less of it than most
which may be why he felt a need to distinguish between them.
This may also be why secretly I believe that Kant favoured time.
Besides, there are the more preferable "delicious burdens."
That's how Whitman regarded time when he called his memories
the "delicious burdens" he carried with him wherever he went.
As if to suggest our existence is our self: an object
passing through space and time,
something that is filled but also fills.

Time is everywhere, defined
in a variety of ways by people who are now
in the past tense.

Outside the winter light is skipping vacantly
across the frozen landscape of the park
a brief alignment of space, in greys and browns.
The atmosphere of the thing is cold. It is January.
What I am looking at is time as it has been displayed to me
A few days after my forty-sixth birthday. It is particular;
at the very least a thing that considers nothing
while I consider a January afternoon
like those you remember, but it isn't the same.

People may say it's a miracle to have seen it,
but I can remember having seen something similar,
so nothing special. What we know *a priori* is a feeling
conjoined, a distant object brought to us by time, light
travelling through all that space only to reveal a frozen park
because I happened to look out the window.

Lately I have come to realize I am no longer young, youth being
something I can only recall, a delicious burden that has been
bestowed upon me as temporal as anything, a sensibility
that has been brought to the forefront of my life randomly,
and unassumingly. Take for instance the following memory:
One day not too long ago my eldest son turned eighteen
and the CBC broadcast the final performance of a band
whose music played in the background for many years.
I remember this. And as my wife and I watched the show and
kids mingled in the back yard, we also witnessed our mortality.
And all we could really know was the now of it: a place
we arrived at so casually simply because we are people
who exist, full of whatever we have gathered into our lives
and our memories that are surely as mortal as anyone.

How Light Pours from the Darkness

Sometimes you can actually see a poem.
Say you are floating in a canoe along
The Humber River one evening
And you notice you are alongside a
Cormorant who is eyeing you —
You feel a series of words
That will capture this moment
Perfectly, a moment you and the
Bird are sharing in the stillness
Of the growing darkness. And you
Feel these words until you can see them
Almost like type on a page, right there
And your son in the back of the boat
Sneezes and the bird disappears
beneath the surface of the water.
Watching the ripples expand from where
The bird vanished, you have an epiphany —
It probably wouldn't have been a very good
Poem anyway, there would have been
Too much artifice to it, it would have
Been too precious, a perfect example
Of a Canadian nature poem. So you
Paddle onward. Further down stream
You look up and notice all the cormorants,
Hundreds of them, perched at the tops
Of the trees growing along the shore.

Off in the Distance

There is a plane in the sky.
It could be a reflection of the plane
I am in, which is also in the sky.
I could be looking around the planet
At myself seated at the window
Of a plane looking off
In the distance at myself.

Afterword
by Tim Conley

> a belief i have that poetry
> happens small and in spaces between
> people and the failures of language
> we are alive in
>
> (from *esp: Accumulation Sonnets*)

I

"He didn't look like a poet," one student said in a flat voice when I asked my contemporary literature class what they had made of Jay MillAr's visit the week before. This happened some years ago, when Jay had come to talk about his unusual book *Mycological Studies* and answer questions from students about what it was like to be a writer in the twenty-first century.

"He didn't look like a poet." My first thought was: *were they expecting a cape?* But then I reflected that in all likelihood they had no idea what to expect, and what they had found in his book probably didn't look like poetry, either, to their eyes. What does Jay MillAr look like? Eerily ageless; pretty much like he did when I first met him in a university pub twenty-five years ago. A steady gaze, a boyish curl of a smile, sandy hair that doesn't seem to need a comb. Like a poker player, or an '80s computer whiz kid who's walked away from it all, or a roadie who has been with the band since the very beginning, or all of the above. He does not look like a poet.

There is something in that.

II

Always on the move, but still in reflection. Whether he is tagging fieldmice or sniffing after mushrooms in London, Ontario and environs, or stalking the streets and streetcars of Toronto, Jay MillAr, man with the instress in his name, likes his rhythms sprung. His muse is Traffic, literal and metaphysical: the way people move, even if we feel we are not moving as we sit in a bus or plane; the way the world moves around us, even as we move with it; the movement of culture, and especially the trafficking of books, his own and those of many others. MillAr's poetry is a kind of sustained consciousness of how movement and inertia are simultaneously experienced, the one an illusion of the other.

Time, one of his most habitual themes, is what underwrites this consciousness. We are always moving through time. When his poems give dates, they are often jokes, and even when not they are receding, not speciously coming into view. In all of his poems the forward momentum neither abates nor pretends that it could.

Boredom offers a kind of case study to which he often returns: what kind of equilibrium is achieved between consciousness and time when one feels bored? This is not the *ennui* at which Baudelaire sneered and which was embraced as a symptom of world-troubled genius by so many decadent poets (and by even more subsequent would-be poets, always in MillAr's field of vision). MillAr's poems typically accept boredom as just another state of mind, but also an opportunity. It may be all very well to recollect, in something called tranquillity, the spontaneous overflow of powerful feelings, but Wordsworth wanted to shut out the world that he complained was too much with him (and he never owned a wristwatch, never mind a smartphone). MillAr never makes such a complaint not only because his experience and sense of movement, time, and mundanity are so historically different from those of poets of the past, but because it is paradoxically in those phenomena that he sees, and shows us, stillness, the flickering instant, the extraordinary.

III

If so many easy shop-labels do point to some significant facet of his work and thought, none wholly encompasses them: "nature poet" (that persistent Romantic self-identification with landscape), "city poet" (cadences of the streetcar and subway, borrowed forms of "I do this, I do that"), "love poet" (the frequency with which one encounters the name "Hazel" makes it an inevitable point of reference, a guiding star by which to navigate), "political poet" (contemptuous of what damage troglodytic governments, like that of Mike Harris, have wrought on communities), "experimental poet" (cough, cough), and even, to some extent, *poète maudit*. The reader of this collection, tripping from conceit to constraint to concrete, will observe that there's more truth than bravado in this statement:

> I would like to disclaim any and all stylistic modes that might box me into anything. I dislike the term experimental (innovative is ok but is also a silly term). I also dislike most of the terms that have ever been used to describe what kind of poetry something is. Isn't it bad enough to call it poetry? I mean, not in the sense that poetry is bad, but in the sense that we shouldn't need some other term there trying to make the poetry more interesting.[i]

Nonetheless, MillAr's influences are unhidden: from Canada,

bill bissett, Gerry Gilbert, Christopher Dewdney, Phil Hall, the Toronto Small Press Group; from the US, Frank O'Hara, Ted Berrigan, John Berryman, and yes, of course, Joe Brainard. Among others — MillAr is always among others, an expanding circle of others. A number of the early works collected here are pastiches and homages, headlong and fun, but his affinities with other writers remain a guiding force even in his more mature writings. The labels don't much matter because MillAr is so unashamed of his loves.

IV

His poetry doesn't wear a cape, either. The poems are self-consciously casual and colloquial, inflected with teasing and an irony blended by punk rock, the New York School, and something about being Canadian. They can be if not "confessional," frank and revealing, less an act of self-aggrandizement than of friendship. That said, "voice" tends to be changeable and decentralized. The tonal register almost always shifts when, speaking of poetry as an institution, his tongue fills his cheek. How's this for lofty:

> In the midst of such an immense, soundless, and high concern
> the shattered rose of insomnia barfs softly
> upon the tax of deathless vulgarity, a quiet spasm of grit,
> feeble and cold on the horizon.

These lines come from "Your Next Hit Single," included in this volume. But that's not the whole story, for MillAr's poem is made up of 100 lines of other poems, lines taken from the grandly titled *100 Great Poems of the Twentieth Century*, edited by Mark Strand (Norton, 2005). Not only can the devil quote scripture, the devil can quote and quote and quote.

A ventriloquism act without a dummy, that's MillAr's poetry. Or perhaps a series of acts, a full variety show. Now on stage — who do you suppose this sounds like:

> if nyte shld end and i awayke shld be
> kyssing thy lips on bended knee
>
> slit mye throat, cut oute mye hearte
> to dye ryte then could be great art
>
> and if its not then ile be dead
> no mre the fear of marriage beds
>
> these pritty eyes no longr wyll i owne
> to see yu walk away, leaving me alowne

Keats as a goth girl, who once shared an apartment with bill bissett. She is Gwendlyn (don't make me sic) Parker, an angry, ribald lyricist with one limited-edition chapbook to her name: *Fuck the World I Want to Get Off* (1996).[ii] So far as I know, MillAr has never publicly acknowledged this thing of darkness his, but at least it might be said that there are precursors to the "ghosts of Jay MillAr" gathered in the book of that title, a book of heteronyms.

While his poems are everywhere explorations of demotic language, MillAr is less interested in representing speech than in representing thought processes, how our minds shuffle, leap, or tumble through the passing of time. This is not to say that the poems aren't ready to be read aloud: that's part of the play, a sense of play that invites the reader to play, too. MillAr is suspicious, to say the least, of wit that is not part of a shared conversation, and any persona he adopts comes with its own self-deflation mechanism. He has even done that impossible thing, invented a laugh track that actually works:

> Some
> wait for people to die some wait for
> people to heal all of us are waiting for
> our indemnification tags. If you take a
> room with no windows they give you $600
> back, but I'm wondering if I can just go
> on holiday with my gameboy. I keep
> forgetting that humans are frames from
> which genitals have been hung by someone
> with an evolutionary sense of humour.
> Ha ha ha ha ha ha ha ha ha ha ha ha![iii]

I don't know about you, but I fall for that one every time.

V

Does "self-published" sound incriminating, or even self-incriminating? Is it worse than wearing white after Labour Day? Is it "unprofessional," or "a bad career move"?

MillAr's first book of poems (which in a 2007 interview he said he feels "neither proud nor embarrassed" about[iv]) was also his start as a publisher, and it is impossible to separate these two roles. *Uranium Kisses Will Knock Your Socks Off* — arguably a title that only a first-time author could love — appeared under the imprint "boondoggle books" (the name would not always be in lower case letters) in 1992. During the visit to my class, he recalled how in his undergraduate days he became interested in hunting down books without proper spines in the library, the books not mass-produced and all too likely to escape notice. This early stalking of shelves developed into a pathology, finding him working for a spell at the Toronto bookseller Contact Editions, getting an MA in English at York University, and later enrolled in a graduate program in library studies at the University of Toronto.[v]

But it's not enough just to consume: that's not the basis for a meaningful, participatory economy. Nor is the economy of literature — which for MillAr is really the same thing as talking about community and relationships — to be left to big publishing companies who, precisely because they are so little committed to anything but the fiscal bottom line, are averse to risk. "How to Write Poetry," a broadside in whose title and thunderous zeal can be heard the banging typewriter of Ezra Pound, concludes:

> dont let any of the corporate
> motherfuckers publish any poetry publish it yrself
> in small sturdy editions that are given away to people
> you know would like it fuck the rest of the world
> theyre as stoopid as you are its just something you do
> writing that is all your opinions will change tomorrow
> anyway[vi]

MillAr's is a pointedly pragmatic answer to Lautréamont's decree that poetry must be made not by one but by everyone. Writing is "just something you do" or, if one prefers, not do, and that choice cannot and should not be falsely delegated to anyone else, least of all the publishing industry.

Poetry is too important *and* too unimportant for that kind

of surrender. As he explained in a kind of manifesto for his press:
> literally, boondoggle means to carry out something useless & trivial acts with the appearance of doing something important. well, if you look at it from another angle, it's like, Oh Well. &this, perhaps is the challenge, to admit that the "important" is trivial or that the "trivial" is important, or maybe they're really well, Oh Well.[vii]

For all the shrugs — as always, that insouciant manner can cause one to miss the earnest energy beneath it (*he didn't look like a poet*) — MillAr is easily among the most tireless people in the Canadian literary scene of the past half-century (*always on the move*). Just looking at a single decade, the Boondoggle years of 1990s, one is staggered by the rate of production: over a dozen titles in 1995 alone. And let's not forget that each copy is produced and distributed by hand. And let's not forget that in the same decade MillAr edited a couple of literary journals, *HIJ* and *B after C*. And let's not forget that he also gave countless readings and contributed to various journals during this time.

Boondoggle became BookThug in 2004, and now as Book*hug it is recognized as one of the most significant poetry presses in North America. Book*hug boasts some 250 titles in its full catalogue, and includes among its diverse list of authors Aisha Sasha John, Phil Hall, bpNichol, Andre Alexis, Helen Guri, Stephen Cain, Lisa Robertson, Erin Wunker, Moez Surani, Steve McCaffery, Lisa Jarnot, Victor Coleman, Kate Eichhorn, Nicole Markotić, Shannon Maguire, Ron Silliman, Marianne Apostolides, Jonathan Ball, Karen MacCormack, and Erin Mouré. Gertrude Stein's declaration "I write for myself and others" could be adjusted to express the BookThug ethos: "I publish myself and others." And let's not forget that in the same decade

MillAr founded the Toronto New School of Writing with Jenny Sampirisi, gave countless readings, and so on and so forth, and fathered two sons with Hazel, until the business more or less became a family affair.

VI

This book is not conceived of as a "greatest hits" album — which would, I hope it is by this point clear, be entirely antithetical to MillAr's poetics — but rather as a cross-section of an oeuvre still growing.[viii] In some ways it might be best to think of it as a naturalist's collection of samples, gathered over many seasons, taken together as a historical document. It is meant to give a sense of the variety and evolution of forms, styles, and interests that have animated Jay MillAr's poetry for close to thirty years.

Animated is, I think, very much the right word. This is a poetry that is alive and sees us and says you, hey you, you are alive, too. And in that moment, we are.

---

i. "Jay MillAr – Timely Irreverence (an interview)." Toronto Quarterly (online, 3 July 2013)

ii. Gwendlyn Parker, *Fuck the World I Want to Get Off: Selected Poems* (Toronto: Boondoggle Books, 1996). Obviously the title has more than one meaning, and it's likewise impossible to read Parker without noticing ironic contradictions.

iii. "Our Journey from Silence" (from this volume).

iv. "12 or 20 questions: with Jay MillAr." rob mclennan's blog (http://robmclennan.blogspot.com) 20 November 2007.

v. And in 2002, he opened Apollinaire's Bookshoppe, an online and sometimes pop-up market of secondhand twentieth-century literature with the memorable slogan, "selling the books no one wants to buy."

vi. "How to Write Poetry" (dated 11/21/1995), included with *i'mnotsurewhati'm-supposedtosay: a boondoggle festo* (Toronto: Boondoggle Books, 1995).

vii. *i'mnotsurewhati'msupposedtosay: a boondoggle festo* (dated 12/20/1995).

viii. In consultation with the author, some very minor corrections have been made to a few poems that will distinguish them from earlier versions.

Books by Jay MillAr

Reflecting both the spirit and history of MillAr's multifarious and industrious publishing, this chronological list includes chapbooks, broadsides, and pamphlets as well as "trade" books, without preferential distinctions.

Uranium Kisses Will Knock Your Socks Off (Toronto: Boondoggle Books, 1992)
greydaze: a luv story (Toronto: Boondoggle Books, 1992)
a pauze for windchymze (Toronto: Boondoggle Books, 1992/3)
All Purpose Frame (Toronto: Boondoggle Books, 1995)
Joe Brainard Is Dead (Toronto: Boondoggle Books, 1995)
A Band Called PREEN (Toronto: No Nothing Press, 1995)
The Night Jerry Garcia Died (Toronto: Boondoggle Books, 1995)
Box of Legs (Toronto: Boondoggle Books, 1995)
A Break in the Clouds (Toronto: Boondoggle Books, 1995)
One Night (Toronto: Boondoggle Books, 1995)
The Overcoat (Toronto: Boondoggle Books, 1995)
"Westerns" (Toronto: Boondoggle Books, 1995)
Meow: Six Cat Poems (Toronto: Boondoggle Books, 1995)
Mountainfuck (with John Barlow and bill bissett; Toronto: Boondoggle Books, 1995)
The Great Relay Race (with Rob Lemon; Toronto: Boondoggle Books, 1995)
Winding Up My Vincent (Toronto: Boondoggle Books, 1995)
i'mnotsurewhati'msupposedtosay: a boondoggle festo (Toronto: Boondoggle Books, 1995)
Lugs (Toronto: Boondoggle Books, 1995)
Across South Western Ontario (Toronto: Boondoggle Books, 1996)
February Love Songs (Toronto: Boondoggle Books, 1996)
On the Fly (Toronto: Boondoggle Books, 1996)
Notes Towards a Poem on Our Honeymoon (Toronto: Boondoggle Books, 1996)
J: a metric system (Toronto: Boondoggle Books, 1996)
Bike poem (Toronto: Boondoggle Books, 1996)
OneWay (Toronto: Boondoggle Books, 1996)

Wrapping paper: on the outskirts of december (Toronto: Boondoggle
  Books, 1996)
Fuck the World I Want to Get Off: Selected Poems (writing as Gwend-
  lyn Parker; Toronto: Boondoggle Books, 1996)
Back Roads & Other Creatures (Toronto: BookThug, 1997)
Horsehair Jacket (Toronto: BookThug, 1997)
Just Like Stealing Smiles from a Baby (Toronto: BookThug, 1998)
Coast All Journ All (Toronto: BookThug, 1998)
Midsts (Toronto: BookThug, 1998)
Psyche List, or maybe I'll just keep going (Toronto: BookThug, 1998)
Sum Lakes (Toronto: BookThug, 1998)
Wrap (Toronto: BookThug, 1998)
Hanging Conversation: A Letter Opened to jwcurry (Toronto: Book-
  Thug, 1998)
The Ghosts of Jay MillAr (Toronto: Coach House Books, 1998/2000)
In Another Shimmering Lifetime: an attempt at memory for you
  (Toronto: BookThug, 2000)
Testing Patterns: Four Seasons (Toronto: BookThug, 2000)
Seven Species of Insect / Four Species of Mushroom (Toronto: Book-
  Thug, 2001)
Appendix to an Appendix: XXVI Fungal Threads (Toronto: Book-
  Thug, 2002)
Mycological Studies (Toronto: Coach House Books, 2002)
Let's Call These Poems St. Clair Avenue (Ottawa: above/ground
  press, 2003)
the small blue (Toronto: BookThug, 2003)
Hijinks: A Sequence from Double Helix (with Stephen Cain; Ottawa:
  above/ground press, 2003)
Pissing Ice: An Anthology of 'New' Canadian Poets (edited by Jon
  Paul Fiorentino and Jay MillAr; Toronto: BookThug, 2004)
False Maps for Other Creatures (Roberts Creek, BC: Nightwood
  Editions, 2005)
Sporatic Growth, being a third season of 26 fungal threads (Vancou-
  ver: Nomados, 2006)
Stitch Decends a Briefcase (Toronto: BookThug, 2006)
Double Helix (with Stephen Cain; Toronto: Mercury, 2006)
Demtened Poems I-X (Mt. Pleasant, ON: Laurel Reed Books, 2007)
the small blue (Montreal: Snare Books, 2007)

Lack Lyrics (Toronto: BookThug, 2007)
Red Wheelbarrow (Toronto: BookThug, 2007)
Woods Pages (Vernon, BC: Greenboathouse Books, 2008)
esp: Accumulation Sonnets (Toronto: BookThug, 2009)
Other Poems (Gibsons, BC: Nightwood Editions, 2010)
Timely Irreverence (Toronto: BookThug, 2011)
The Shiny Things (Ottawa: above/ground press, 2012)
Timely Irreverence (Gibsons, BC: Nightwood Editions, 2013)
I Could Have Pretended to Be Better than You: Seven Poems (Toronto: BookThug, 2014)
Another Poem About Time Written At The Onset of Middle Age (Toronto: Someone Editions, 2018)
Off in the Distance (Wilmington, NC: Happy Monk Press, 2018)

Notes to the Poems

Part One: The Years of Stitches and Staples (1992-1999)
"Cartographers World": first published in *Uranium kisses will knock your socks off* (Boondoggle Books, 1992).
"Poem": first published in *A Break in the Clouds* (Boondoggle Books, 1995).
"Joe Brainard Is Dead": first appeared as *Joe Brainard Is Dead* (Toronto: Boondoggle Books, 1995).
"A Fact": first published in *Box of Legs* (Boondoggle Books, 1995).
"Errata": first published in *One Night* (Boondoggle Books, 1995).
"Morning Sky": first published in *Across South Western Ontario* (Boondoggle Books, 1996).
"To My Illustrious Career": first published in *On the Fly* (Boondoggle Books, 1996).
[Yawning again, waking up again]: taken from Book IV of *J: a metric system* (Boondoggle Books, 1996).
[You make me realize]: taken from Book VI of *J: a metric system* (Boondoggle Books, 1996).
"Space Travel" first published in *Notes Towards a Poem on Our Honeymoon* (Boondoggle Books, 1996).
"Back Seat News": first published in *Sum Lakes* (BookThug, 1998).
[Maybe we weren't so unimaginable]: taken from *Midsts* (BookThug, 1998).
"imaginary tombstones": first published in *Midsts* (BookThug, 1998).
[bad days always begin the night before]: taken from *Just Like Stealing Smiles from a Baby* (BookThug, 1998).

Part Two: Seriously Taken (2000-2014)
"Tree Culture — Some Field Notes" and "Trees": first published in *The Ghosts of Jay MillAr* (Coach House Books; though the book lists 1998 as its publication date, it actually appeared in 2000). These writings are attributed to Conwenna Stokes the first of MillAr's five heteronyms (or ghosts) gathered in this book.
"Lysdexia in Sunlight": first published in *Back Roads & Other Creatures* (BookThug, 1997); later attributed to Alex Cayce in *The Ghosts of Jay MillAr* (Coach House Books, 1998/2000).

"Seasonal Drift": attributed to Alex Cayce in *The Ghosts of Jay MillAr* (Coach House Books, 1998/2000).

"Critique of the Dying": attributed to H. Azel in *The Ghosts of Jay MillAr* (Coach House Books, 1998/2000).

"In Another Shimmering Lifetime": first appeared as *In Another Shimmering Lifetime: an attempt at memory for you* (BookThug, 2000), with MillAr credited as author and this note: "*To commemorate the passing of ten years since the occurace* [sic] *of the described events.*" Later attributed to H. Azel in *The Ghosts of Jay MillAr* (Coach House Books, 1998/2000).

"Perfectly Ordinary Dream #1620 (August 17, 1925)" "Perfectly Ordinary Dream #1962 (September 17, 1985)," and "Perfectly Ordinary Dream #4127 (March 30, 1928)": attributed to James Llar in *The Ghosts of Jay MillAr* (Coach House Books, 1998/2000).

"What in the World is Coming to": attributed to John Elliott in *The Ghosts of Jay MillAr* (Coach House Books, 1998/2000).

"Fly Agaric (amanita muscaria)" and "Destroying Angel (amanita virosa)": first published in *Seven Species of Insect / Four Species of Mushroom* (BookThug, 2001).

"False Morels," "As Seen from Above," and "As Seen from Below": first published in *Mycological Studies* (Coach House Books, 2002).

"7 Fungal Threads": a selection of seven of a series of twenty-six poems, which first appeared in *Appendix to an Appendix: XXVI Fungal Threads* (BookThug, 2002) just prior to their publication in *Mycological Studies* (Coach House Books, 2002).

"Fact's Mile": first published in *False Maps for Other Creatures* (Nightwood Editions, 2005).

"Nearby, Lakes": first appeared in *Queen Street Quarterly*; subsequently included in *False Maps for Other Creatures* (Nightwood Editions, 2005).

"Carve," "Data," "Home," and "Privacy" all come from *Double Helix*, a collaboration with Stephen Cain (Mercury, 2006).

"dense joke," "drowned notions of passed," and "bizarrely tunes itself" first appeared in *the small blue* (BookThug, 2003), later republished by Snare Books (2007), a collection of 79 numbered poems. At public readings from the book, MillAr would invite the audience to call out numbers and he would read the corresponding poems.

"Lack Lyric I," "Lack Lyric IV," and "Lack Lyric V": drawn from *Lack Lyrics* (BookThug, 2007).

The seven sonnets ("forlorn falls of autumn"; "oh so this is your sidewalk"; "the bits of light that don't repeat"; "the sun goes down how narrative"; "star covered seams of church daze"; "skim elk clop soda"; "in the future manifesto") all first appeared in *esp: Accumulation Sonnets* (BookThug, 2009).

"Lake Ontario Suite": first appeared in *Prairie Fire*; later included in *Other Poems* (Nightwood Editions, 2010).

"On Vocal Technique": first published in *Other Poems* (Nightwood Editions, 2010).

"Wood Pages": first published as a limited chapbook, *Woods| Pages* (Greenboathouse Books, 2008) and later reprinted in *Other Poems* (Nightwood Editions, 2010).

"Lift": first published in *Timely Irreverence* (Nightwood Editions, 2013).

"The Lyrics to Your Next Hit Single": first published in *Timely Irreverence* (Nightwood Editions, 2013).

"More Trouble with the Obvious": first appeared in *THIS Magazine*; later reprinted in *Demtented Poems I-X* (Laurel Reed Books, 2007) and *Timely Irreverence* (Nightwood Editions, 2013).

"Timely Irreverence": first published as a "Moments Café" broadside (BookThug, 2011); later included in *Timely Irreverence* (Nightwood Editions, 2013).

Part Three: New Poems (2014-18)

"On Time": first published in *I Could Have Pretended to Be Better than You: Seven Poems* (BookThug, 2014).

"Gathered for the Purpose," "Conceptual Poetry," "A Sentient Being Rises from the Sea," "The Nature," and "Our Journey from Silence" are all unpublished poems from *Demtented Poems*, a manuscript of 100 interconnected poems that was harvested from by Silas White to create the book *Timely Irreverence* (Nightwood Editions, 2015). "Conceptual Poetry" was first published in *The Puritan* in 2016.

"The Shiny Things": first appeared as *The Shiny Things* (above/ground press, 2012). This piece was composed while cataloguing sections of the personal library of Canadian scholar Barbara Godard for York University Special Collections. The titles in the work are all taken from Ted Berrigan's poem "Rusty Nails" found in his book *In the Early Morning Rain*; these titles had originally been given to Berrigan as a list by Ron Padgett, and Berrigan assigned random found texts to them to create what he described as a "novel in miniature." In this poem, the titles from Berrigan's work are rendered in reverse order, and found text from twenty-seven different books on various subjects from Godard's library has been placed randomly and somewhat automatically beneath them. It is unlikely that Berrigan or Godard ever met, or thought about each other, but they share a space in "The Shiny Things" using text neither of them (or the present author for that matter) composed.

"Another Poem About Time Written at the Onset of Middle Age": first appeared as *Another Poem About Time Written at the Onset of Middle Age* (Little Letterpress, 2018).

"How Light Pours from the Darkness": first published in *The Puritan* in 2016.

"Off in the Distance": first published as part of "Memories of Macedonia" on the blog Kornkammer (Denmark) in 2018; also published as Postcard Series #2 by Happy Monk Press (Wilmington, NC) in 2018.

Acknowledgements

Author's Acknowledgements

First of all, much love and gratitude to Hazel, Reid and Cole for joining me in this adventure, and for their significant contributions toward defining me as a person and as a writer. Heartfelt thanks to Tim Conley for spearheading this project, which has revitalized my belief that I can engage with poetry as much as I engage with publishing, made me feel both young and old, and has reminded me of something that I can't really forget because it's all around me. To those independent Canadian publishers who have published my work in the past, my thanks for your support then and now, and for allowing us to select from your publications to create this volume. I'd also like to thank Stephen Cain for allowing us to select work from *Double Helix*. And of course my thanks to Brian Kaufman and Karen Green at Anvil Press for their enthusiasm in taking on and publishing *I Could Have Pretended to Be Better Than You*. And lastly, my thanks to anyone who has been reading my work over the years. Whether you are at arm's length or many kilometres away, I appreciate your thoughtful attention.

Editor's Acknowledgements

Thanks to John Shoesmith and Danielle Van Wagner at the Thomas Fisher Rare Book Library for their patient assistance; to Stephen Cain and Adam Dickinson for thoughtful conversations about this project; to those editors and publishers who have given permission to reprint work included here: rob mclennan, Alana Wilcox (Coach House Books), Leigh Nash (Invisible Publishing), and Silas White (Nightwood Editions); to Anvil Press for taking it on; and to Jay, of course, for reasons that are as obvious as they are many.

About the Author:

Jay MillAr is the author of several books, including *Mycological Studies, the small blue, esp: accumulation sonnets* and *Other Poems*. His most recent book is *Timely Irreverence*. He is also the author of many privately published editions, including *Lack Lyrics*, which tied to win the 2008 bpNichol Chapbook Award. Jay is the co-publisher at Book*hug Press, an independent award-winning publishing house; he also curates Apollinaire's Bookshoppe, a virtual bookstore that specializes in the books that no one wants to buy. For many years he taught poetry/poetics at Toronto New School of Writing. Jay lives and works in Toronto with his partner Hazel and their two sons Reid and Cole.